D1739260

# AN INTRODUCTION TO DECISION LOGIC TABLES

# An Introduction to
# Decision Logic Tables

**HERMAN McDANIEL**

Associate Director
The ADP Management Training Center
U.S. Civil Service Commission

JOHN WILEY & SONS, INC. NEW YORK · LONDON · SYDNEY

# Preface

This book makes no pretense of being a definitive work. It is what its name indicates—an introduction. As such it is hoped that it will fill a void that has long existed in the literature available on decision logic tables.

Except for the section dealing with types of table, the rules and examples appearing in the text are for decision tables in limited-entry format, the type most commonly used. No attempt has been made to explain advanced theories; however, for those who wish to explore them independently, a bibliography is provided in Appendix C.

The glossary (Appendix B) defines terms that might be unfamiliar to the reader.

The progression of the text is such that a working knowledge of decision tables can be acquired in only a few hours, and valuable experience can be gained by working the exercises in Appendix A. The material can be applied to any of several situations:

1. It can be used for individual study of the basics of decision logic tables.
2. It can be used as a supplement to the documentation of existing programming or systems-analysis courses.
3. It can serve as the basic text (or course material) for formal classroom training in the introduction of decision logic tables.

Any undertaking such as writing this book is always more successful when the author receives assistance and cooperation from others knowledgeable in the field. I wish to express my sincere appreciation to the following individuals, each of whom in his own way has contributed greatly to the finished manuscript: James T. O'Brien, Howard Fletcher, Jacqueline P. Davis, Ruth Felker, and Alan Wenberg, all of the U.S. Bureau of the Census, Washington, D.C.; Park F. Anderson, Jr., U.S. Civil Service Commission, Washington, D.C.; Norman Dirks, National Security Agency, Fort Meade, Maryland; William G. Mister, University of California, Berkeley, California; and Wesley H. Cowley, Analysts International Corporation, Washington, D.C. Special thanks are due also to Mrs. Florence Bernhardt for typing the manuscript.

*Herman McDaniel*

Washington, D.C.
April, 1968

# Contents

# AN INTRODUCTION TO DECISION LOGIC TABLES

# 1

---

# Introduction and
# Basic Rules

## WHY DECISION LOGIC TABLES?

Decision logic tables have something for everyone—the programmer, the supervisor, the procedural writer, the systems analyst—even technical writers and management personnel.

Historically flowcharts and/or narratives have been used to structure the logic of a computer problem. These are fine so long as the problem remains simple and straightforward. But when interactions among the various conditions can exist, how can one be certain that he has considered every possible applicable combination? Indeed, one of the most serious problems facing the computer user today is inadequate documentation. In using either flowcharts or narratives, one can become "bogged down" in even a moderately complex problem.

Unlike flowcharts, which may be as detailed or simple as the programmer desires, and which often reflect his logical thinking ability and analytical powers without necessarily being complete or concise, decision tables force one to be thorough and concise. Decision tables, when properly used, demand that all combina-

1

tions of conditions be considered and allow superfluous or irrelevant tests to be deleted.

Once a program has been documented in decision table form it is easy to update the documentation whenever changes in the program are required. This is not so for programs using flowchart documentation. Whereas flowcharts and narratives follow a continuous sequence from beginning to end, decision tables are individually prepared; hence a new "Table 23" could be substituted for the original "Table 23" without disrupting the remainder of the documentation.

Flowcharts and narratives often show only the logic of the problem and serve as documentation once the job is completed. Decision tables do not cease to work once the logic is structured; they may be processed by the computer to generate portions of the actual program.

Decision tables are easy to learn in a short time. In a three-hour session a person may learn decision table techniques sufficiently well to commence working with them. Of course, true efficiency comes only with experience.

In one case a programmer was leaving IBM in a week and was asked to document seven of his programs before leaving. If he had used conventional flowcharts the job would have taken three weeks. The programmer was given less than two hours of training on decision logic tables and then proceeded to write documentation for all seven programs—in two days.

In another case the U.S. Air Force Automatic Resupply Logistics System at Norton Air Force Base, California, had a very complex file-maintenance program. More than six man-years had been spent in an unsuccessful attempt to define the problem with flowcharts and narratives. Then, in 1958, it was decided that an attempt would be made to define the problem using decision logic tables. Four analysts were assigned to the job. They spent the first week establishing their decision table format and criteria. Three weeks later (after 12 man-weeks) the problem was defined.

The U.S. Civil Service Commission's ADP (Automatic Data Processing) Management Training Center now includes half-day sessions in decision logic tables in its various courses for systems analysts. Other government agencies are teaching decision tables in their beginning programmer courses. Many specification writers are being taught decision table techniques and are requested to present their specifications in decision table form to prevent the misunderstandings, due to communication difficulties, that often occur between the technical writer and the programmer when narrative job specifications are used.

Indeed, decision logic tables offer something to everyone.

## THE LOGIC OF DECISION LOGIC TABLES

A decision logic table is simply a tabular display of all elements of a problem from conception to solution. The table shows all conditions affecting the situation at hand and the relationships that exist among the various conditions. The table further indicates which action or actions are appropriate for each set of circumstances.

The logic used in decision tables is similar to that which you use every day, whether you are computer-oriented or not.

Figure 1.1 shows a table of health-insurance premium rates. In determining the premium only two elements of information are required: the age of the individual and his state of health.

| AGE | STATE OF HEALTH | | | |
|---|---|---|---|---|
|  | EXCEL | GOOD | FAIR | POOR |
| Under 30 | 1.28 | 1.53 | 2.00 | 2.73 |
| 30–40 | 1.82 | 2.13 | 2.53 | 3.43 |
| 40–50 | 2.52 | 2.94 | 3.46 | 5.28 |
| 50–60 | 3.28 | 3.92 | 4.84 | 8.74 |
| 60+ | 5.23 | 6.44 | 7.60 | 10.94 |

*Figure 1.1*

The logic for using the table can be stated as follows: "If the applicant is in a certain age bracket *and* if his state of health is so-and-so, then the amount of his premium is $X.XX per month." This simple table contains sufficient information to ascertain the premium for any applicant. Mr. Gregory is 47 years old and in excellent health. His situation might be stated thus: "If applicant is between ages of 40 and 50 and if his state of health is excellent, then his premium will be $2.52 per month."

Decision logic tables are just as clear and concise and are capable of showing meaningful relationships in a similar manner. They are, in fact, based on the same "if . . . then . . ." concept. The "if" area is made up of all conditions or tests that are required to determine the conclusion or actions (the "then" area).

## THE ELEMENTS OF A TABLE

In limited-entry form a decision table has four major sections, as shown in Figure 1.2.

The upper left quadrant is the *condition stub*. This area should contain (in question form) all those conditions being examined for a particular problem segment.

The lower left quadrant is the *action stub*. This area should contain in simple narrative form all possible actions resulting from the conditions listed above.

The upper right quadrant is called the *condition entry* section. It is here that the questions asked in the condition stub area will be answered and all possible *combinations* of these responses will be developed. Responses are restricted to "Y" to indicate yes, "N" to indicate no. If no response is indicated it may be assumed that the condition was not tested in that particular combination.

The remaining quadrant is the *action entry* portion of the table. The appropriate actions resulting from the various combinations of responses to conditions above will be indicated here.

| CONDITION<br>STUB | CONDITION<br>ENTRY |
|---|---|
| ACTION<br>STUB | ACTION<br>ENTRY |

*Figure 1.2*

The only permissible entry here is an "X" next to a listed action to indicate "Take this action." A blank opposite an action in a given column may be interpreted as "Do not take the action shown." One or more actions may be indicated for each combination of condition responses.

The various combinations of responses to conditions shown in the condition entry portion of the table and their resulting actions are called rules or paths. Each is given a number for identification purposes in the *rule header* portion of the table.

One other element each table requires is a means of distinguishing it from all other tables in a given job: a name. The name (called the *table header*) should appear above the condition stub.

The skeleton outline shown in Figure 1.3 shows all basic elements. Note that the condition half of the table is separated from the action half by a horizontal double line. A double vertical line separates the stubs from the entry portions of the table. Because the number of conditions and actions varies from table to table and the number of rules is flexible, these double lines cannot usually be preprinted on the decision table form, but must be drawn by the person who constructs the table. They are an invaluable aid in reading the tables.

The elements are all incorporated in the simple table shown in

TABLE HEADER              RULE HEADER

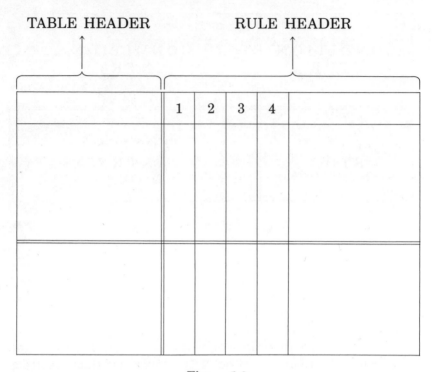

*Figure 1.3*

Figure 1.4. This table represents the following situation. A credit clerk in a wholesale house that deals in small appliances has the responsibility of approving or disapproving incoming credit orders. Of course, in approving or disapproving an order he must apply certain standards. If an order is for less than $700.00 it is to be automatically approved. If an order is for more than $700.00 the clerk checks the records to learn the past pay record of the ordering firm. If the firm has not paid for its prior orders in a satisfactory manner the order is referred to the credit manager for final disposition. However, if the clerk finds that the past pay record of the firm is satisfactory he may approve the order.

From the specifications it is easy to see that three tests will be required: credit limit, pay experience, and special clearance.

These are the conditions for the table. There are only two possible actions in this case: either to approve or disapprove the order. The various pertinent combinations of the conditions and actions may be represented by four rules. Rule 1 may read, "*If* the credit level is okay, *then* approve the order." Rule 2 states, "*If* the credit limit is not okay but the firm's pay record is favorable, *then* approve the order." Rule 3 may be interpreted as "*If* the credit level is *not* okay and the firm's record of payment is *not* okay, but the credit manager does give special clearance, *then* approve the order." Rule 4 says, "*If* credit level is *not* okay, past pay experience is *not* favorable, and special clearance *was not* obtained from the credit manager, *then* disapprove the order."

Notice that if testing of a condition is not necessary in a given situation the rule entry space for that particular rule is left blank. In rule 1 on the credit table, if the credit limit is okay the order may be approved without testing conditions 2 and 3.

Since this table contains a rule covering each possible applicable situation, it could be used to process any number of incoming orders. Probably most orders would fall into the

| DECISION LOGIC TABLE | | Job *CREDIT*  Date *10-10-65* | | | | | | | | |
| --- | --- | --- | --- | --- | --- | --- | --- | --- | --- | --- |
| | | Prepared by *G. MARKUS* | | | | | | | | |
| *CREDIT* | | 1 | 2 | 3 | 4 | | | | | |
| *IS CREDIT LIMIT OKAY ?* | | Y | N | N | N | | | | | |
| *FAVORABLE PAYMENT RECORD ?* | | | Y | N | N | | | | | |
| *SPECIAL CLEARANCE OBTAINED?* | | | | Y | N | | | | | |
| *APPROVE ORDER* | | X | X | X | | | | | | |
| *DISAPPROVE ORDER* | | | | | X | | | | | |

*Figure 1.4*

categories reflected in rules 1 and 2, but the table shown covers any situation that might arise in credit approval.

## TYPES OF TABLES

### Limited-Entry Tables

In general usage there are three types of tables. Limited-entry tables (of which Figure 1.4 is an example) are by far the most widely used type. In this form the rules regarding the placement of information in each of the four quadrants are fixed and inflexible. The condition *and* its state or value must be restricted to the condition stub; the condition entry may show only the response "Y," "N," or a blank. Likewise the specific actions must be fully identified within the action stub; permissible notations in the action entry section are limited to "X" or a blank. In short, restrictions dictate that entries normally contained in one quadrant may not overflow or extend into another quadrant when a table is in limited-entry format.

Figure 1.5 shows certain population characteristics in limited-entry format.

Although limited-entry tables tend to be longer than the other two types, they are built on binary logic patterns, which are especially well suited to computer applications.

### Extended-Entry Tables

In extended-entry tables the condition stub serves only to identify the variables to be tested, while the condition entry must define the value or state of the variable. This value may be absolute or related to another value. Likewise in such a table the action stub only names an action; the action entry will give the specifics for the action named. Figure 1.6 shows in extended-entry form exactly the same information shown in Figure 1.5.

Use of the extended-entry format tends to decrease the number of items listed in both the condition stub and the action stub,

| DECISION LOGIC TABLE | Job *POP. CHAR-ACTERISTICS* Date<br>Prepared by *FOX* | | | |
|---|---|---|---|---|
| *RACE / SEX* | | | | |
| | *1* | *2* | *3* | *4* |
| *IS PERSON WHITE ?* | *Y* | *Y* | *N* | *N* |
| *IS PERSON MALE ?* | *Y* | *N* | *Y* | *N* |
| *TALLY CAUCASIAN MALE* | *X* | | | |
| *TALLY CAUCASIAN FEMALE* | | *X* | | |
| *TALLY NON-CAUCASIAN MALE* | | | *X* | |
| *TALLY NON-CAUCASIAN FEMALE* | | | | *X* |
| | | | | |
| | | | | |
| | | | | |

**Figure 1.5**

| DECISION LOGIC TABLE | Job *POP CHAR-ACTERISTICS* Date<br>Prepared by *FOX* | | | |
|---|---|---|---|---|
| *RACE / SEX* | | | | |
| | *1* | *2* | *3* | *4* |
| *PERSONS RACE ?* | *CAU* | *CAU* | *NON-CAU* | *NON-CAU* |
| *PERSONS SEX ?* | *MALE* | *FEMALE* | *MALE* | *FEMALE* |
| *TALLY* | *A* | *B* | *C* | *D* |
| | | | | |
| | | | | |
| | | | | |
| | | | | |
| | | | | |
| *LEGEND :* | | | | |
| *TALLY A — CAUCASIAN MALES* | | | | |
| *TALLY B — CAUCASIAN FEMALES* | | | | |
| *TALLY C — NON-CAUCASIAN MALES* | | | | |
| *TALLY D — NON-CAUCASIAN FEMALES* | | | | |
| | | | | |
| | | | | |

**Figure 1.6**

9

thus compressing the size of the table vertically. It also offers the possibility of considering more than two responses to a given condition. However, it is often necessary to convert extended-entry tables to limited-entry form if they are to be programmed.

### Mixed-Entry Tables

When limited-entry form and extended-entry form are combined into a single table, the resulting table is said to be in mixed-entry form. Even though these two forms may be combined, one form must be used exclusively within each horizontal row of a table. Figure 1.7 depicts the previously used population-characteristics tables (Figs. 1.5 and 1.6) in mixed-entry format.

| DECISION LOGIC TABLE | Job *POP. CHAR-ACTERISTICS* Date<br>Prepared by *FOX* | | | |
|---|---|---|---|---|
| *RACE / SEX* | | | | |
| | *1* | *2* | *3* | *4* |
| *PERSONS RACE ?* | *CAU* | *CAU* | *NON-CAU* | *NON-CAU* |
| *PERSONS SEX ?* | *MALE* | *FEMALE* | *MALE* | *FEMALE* |
| *TALLY CAUCASIAN MALE* | *X* | | | |
| *TALLY CAUCASIAN FEMALE* | | *X* | | |
| *TALLY NON-CAUCASIAN MALE* | | | *X* | |
| *TALLY NON-CAUCASIAN FEMALE* | | | | *X* |
| | | | | |
| | | | | |

*Figure 1.7*

# 2

---

# Learn through Examples

From what you have learned thus far, convert the following narrative to a limited-entry decision logic table. Do not turn the page until you have finished your table. A solution with explanation appears in Figure 2.1.

## The Situation

A steamship line has a reservations and ticket counter where customers make reservations and purchase cruise tickets. If a customer requests cabin class accommodations and a cabin is available, issue a cabin class ticket and subtract one from the total number of cabins (so as not to oversell the capacity of the ship). If cabin class accommodations are not available, place the customer's name on a waiting list for cabin class. If the customer requests tourist accommodations and they are available, issue a tourist class ticket. You must also remember to subtract one from tourist availability. If tourist class is requested but is not available, place the customer's name on a waiting list for tourist class. For the purposes of this problem, if the class initially requested is not available, there is no possibility of assigning an alternate class.

11

| DECISION LOGIC TABLE | Job *ADV. PROM.*   Date *9-22-65* Prepared by   *JIM FRANTZ* |
|---|---|

*CRUISE*

| | 1 | 2 | 3 | 4 | | | | | | | |
|---|---|---|---|---|---|---|---|---|---|---|---|
| IS REQUEST FOR CABIN CLASS ? | Y | Y | N | N | | | | | | | |
| IS CABIN AVAILABLE ? | Y | N | | | | | | | | | |
| TOURIST AVAILABLE ? | | | Y | N | | | | | | | |
| ISSUE CABIN TICKET, SUB 1 FROM TOTAL | X | | | | | | | | | | |
| PLACE ON CABIN WAITING LIST | | X | | | | | | | | | |
| ISSUE TOURIST TICKET, SUB 1 FROM TOTAL | | | X | | | | | | | | |
| PLACE ON TOURIST WAITING LIST | | | | X | | | | | | | |

*Figure 2.1*

### Solutions

One possible solution is shown in Figure 2.1; others may be just as valid as long as they cover the same situations.

By using the logic that was used on the earlier population-characteristics tables we can effectively combine two conditions into one. Since there are only two possible classes of travel it is not necessary to ask, "Is the request for cabin class?" followed by, "Is the request for tourist class?" Ask about only one class. Process the "yes" responses to the condition for the class being asked about; process the "no" responses to that condition as if they were "yes" responses to the other class. Note that in this table the condition asks, "Is request for cabin class?" The "yes" responses are processed for cabin class availability, cabin class ticket, and cabin class waiting list. The "no" responses to the same condition are interpreted as a "yes" response to the un-asked "Is request for tourist class?" The subsequent check for space availability is for tourist class; the ticket issued or waiting list used is also for tourist class.

Since each time a ticket is sold one must be subtracted from the number of tickets available in that particular class, the issuance of the ticket and the subtraction are performed as an action packet. Of course a separate issue-and-subtract packet is needed for each class in limited-entry form. Actions may be combined *only* if, each time one of the actions is performed, the other is also required.

The table as shown contains in the condition entry portion one blank area in each rule column. This is because the response to the first condition affects the relevance of a subsequent condition in every instance. In rules 1 and 2 "Is request for cabin class?" is answered "yes." Since there is no alternative class option in the problem there is obviously no reason to check for tourist availability in these two cases. Conversely, rules 3 and 4 have a response of "no" to "Is request for cabin class?"—indicating that the request is then for tourist class. In these paths it is irrelevant to ask about the availability of cabin class.

In situations such as these, in which the answer to a condition affects the relevance of a subsequent condition (the answer to a condition makes later conditions in the same path either irrelevant or impossible), the two conditions are said to have logical interaction.

It can be safely stated that the decision table shown as Figure 2.1 covers all relevant or applicable situations indicated by the job specifications.

## DETERMINING MAXIMUM TABLE SIZE

In limited-entry format each condition has one of two possible answers: yes or no. Based on this fact, the number of conditions in such a table dictates the maximum number of rules possible. The number of conditions in the table becomes the exponent of the number 2 to determine the possible number of rules. For example, a table having three conditions would have $2^3$ (or 8) rules possible. Note that for each condition added to the table, its possible size doubles. A table with four conditions would have $2^4$ (or 16) possible rules.

## A METHOD OF ELIMINATING IRRELEVANT TESTS

A table will require the maximum number of rules only when no logical interaction among the various conditions is involved. When logical interaction is involved the table will not use the maximum number of rules possible. The cruise table in Figure 2.1 uses only four rules, yet it covers all relevant situations.

If the fact that there is logical interaction is ignored, the table for the cruise may look like the one shown in Figure 2.2. Remov-

| DECISION LOGIC TABLE | Job *ADV. PROM.*   Date *9-21-65*<br>Prepared by  *JIM FRANTZ* | | | | | | | | | |
|---|---|---|---|---|---|---|---|---|---|---|
| *CRUISE* | | | | | | | | | | |
| | 1 | 2 | 3 | 4 | 5 | 6 | 7 | 8 | | |
| IS REQUEST FOR CABIN CLASS ? | Y | Y | Y | Y | N | N | N | N | | |
| IS CABIN AVAILABLE ? | Y | Y | N | N | Y | Y | N | N | | |
| TOURIST AVAILABLE ? | Y | N | Y | N | Y | N | Y | N | | |
| ISSUE CABIN TICKET, SUB 1 FROM TOTAL | X | X | | | | | | | | |
| PLACE ON CABIN WAITING LIST | | | X | X | | | | | | |
| ISSUE TOURIST TICKET, SUB 1 FROM TOTAL | | | | | X | | X | | | |
| PLACE ON TOURIST WAITING LIST | | | | | | X | | X | | |
| | | | | | | | | | | |
| | | | | | | | | | | |
| | | | | | | | | | | |

*Figure 2.2*

ing irrelevant tests in such a table is very easy. If two rules result in the same action (or actions) and there is only one difference in their responses, the condition for which the responses are different should not be tested. For example, rules 1 and 2 both result in the same action. Both rules have "yes" in response to condition 1; both rules have "yes" in response to condition 2. In response to condition 3 rule 1 has "yes" and rule 2 has "no." Whether condition 3 is answered "yes" or "no," the resulting action will be the same. Therefore why test condition 3 in these two paths? Now notice what the third condition concerns: why test for tourist availability when the request is for cabin class and cabin class is available?

Rules 1 and 2 can be combined into a single rule in a new table, leaving blank the condition having different responses. This has been done in Figure 2.3. Rules 3 and 4 result in the same action, and their only difference is in response to condition 3. They can also be combined into a single new rule if the response area for condition 3 is left blank. The new rule is added to the new table in Figure 2.4. Rules 5 and 6 do not result in the same action, but

| DECISION LOGIC TABLE | Job *ADV. PROM.*　Date *9-21-65* Prepared by　*JIM FRANTZ* | | | | | | | | | |
|---|---|---|---|---|---|---|---|---|---|---|
| CRUISE | | | | | | | | | | |
| | *1-2* | | | | | | | | | |
| IS REQUEST FOR CABIN CLASS ? | Y | | | | | | | | | |
| IS CABIN AVAILABLE ? | Y | | | | | | | | | |
| TOURIST AVAILABLE ? | | | | | | | | | | |
| ISSUE CABIN TICKET, SUB 1 FROM TOTAL | X | | | | | | | | | |
| PLACE ON CABIN WAITING LIST | | | | | | | | | | |
| ISSUE TOURIST TICKET, SUB 1 FROM TOTAL | | | | | | | | | | |
| PLACE ON TOURIST WAITING LIST | | | | | | | | | | |
| | | | | | | | | | | |
| | | | | | | | | | | |

*Figure 2.3*

rules 5 and 7 do. Their only difference is in their response to condition 2. Combine them into a new rule and show a blank in the response area for condition 2. The only two rules remaining are 6 and 8. Can they be combined? They have but one difference (in response to condition 2) and they result in the same action. They may be combined if the response area for condition 2 is left blank in the new rule.

Figure 2.5 shows all the combinations discussed above. The old rule numbers have been used here to emphasize the combinations; once the table has been simplified as far as possible, the

**DECISION LOGIC TABLE**

Job ADV. PROM.   Date 9-21-65
Prepared by JIM FRANTZ

CRUISE

| | 1-2 | 3-4 | | | | | | | |
|---|---|---|---|---|---|---|---|---|---|
| IS REQUEST FOR CABIN CLASS ? | Y | Y | | | | | | | |
| IS CABIN AVAILABLE ? | Y | N | | | | | | | |
| TOURIST AVAILABLE ? | | | | | | | | | |
| ISSUE CABIN TICKET, SUB 1 FROM TOTAL | X | | | | | | | | |
| PLACE ON CABIN WAITING LIST | | X | | | | | | | |
| ISSUE TOURIST TICKET, SUB 1 FROM TOTAL | | | | | | | | | |
| PLACE ON TOURIST WAITING LIST | | | | | | | | | |
| | | | | | | | | | |
| | | | | | | | | | |
| | | | | | | | | | |

*Figure 2.4*

**DECISION LOGIC TABLE**

Job ADV. PROM.   Date 9-21-65
Prepared by JIM FRANTZ

CRUISE

| | 1-2 | 3-4 | 5-7 | 6-8 | | | | | |
|---|---|---|---|---|---|---|---|---|---|
| IS REQUEST FOR CABIN CLASS ? | Y | Y | N | N | | | | | |
| IS CABIN AVAILABLE ? | Y | N | | | | | | | |
| TOURIST AVAILABLE ? | | | Y | N | | | | | |
| ISSUE CABIN TICKET, SUB 1 FROM TOTAL | X | | | | | | | | |
| PLACE ON CABIN WAITING LIST | | X | | | | | | | |
| ISSUE TOURIST TICKET, SUB 1 FROM TOTAL | | | X | | | | | | |
| PLACE ON TOURIST WAITING LIST | | | | X | | | | | |
| | | | | | | | | | |
| | | | | | | | | | |

*Figure 2.5*

16

rules should be renumbered from left to right as 1, 2, 3, 4. This is exactly how the table was simplified to the stage shown earlier in Figure 2.1.

## ANOTHER EXERCISE

### *The Situation*

A magazine publisher has just run a promotional subscription campaign in which customers are urged to subscribe for one year or two years. When a subscription is received, if it is on a special order form indicating that it was a result of the campaign, it is to be tagged "promotional"; if not on the special form the subscription is to be tagged "regular." If the subscription is for one year it is to be so tagged; if the subscription is for two years it should be tagged "two years." Those orders enclosing payment are to be tagged "paid"; the others will be tagged "bill." Those subscriptions for city delivery will be tagged "bulk mail"; those for delivery outside the city will be tagged "single mail." The various conditions will have no logical interaction.

### *The Solution*

One possible solution is shown in Figure 2.6. Since the conditions are not logically interacting, in your solution you should have used 16 ($2^4$) rules.

In tables having no logical interaction there is a fixed relationship between the various conditions and the responses in the different rule columns. One way to be sure that the table includes all possible combinations is to order the responses in the following manner. The responses to condition 1 will always be half "yes" and half "no," with the "yes" answers grouped together and the "no" answers grouped together. Condition 2 will show the responses broken into groupings of one-fourth the total number of rules, "yes" answers being equal to one-fourth the total number of rules, followed by the same number of "no's" grouped together, followed by another grouping of "yes" responses, fol-

| DECISION LOGIC TABLE | | Job *MAGAZINE* Date | Prepared by *MORTON* |

*SUBSCRIPTIONS*

| | 1 | 2 | 3 | 4 | 5 | 6 | 7 | 8 | 9 | 10 | 11 | 12 | 13 | 14 | 15 | 16 |
|---|---|---|---|---|---|---|---|---|---|---|---|---|---|---|---|---|
| *PROMOTIONAL ?* | Y | Y | Y | Y | Y | Y | Y | Y | N | N | N | N | N | N | N | N |
| *FOR ONE YEAR ?* | Y | Y | Y | Y | N | N | N | N | Y | Y | Y | Y | N | N | N | N |
| *PAYMENT ENCLOSED?* | Y | Y | N | N | Y | Y | N | N | Y | Y | N | N | Y | Y | N | N |
| *FOR CITY DELIVERY?* | Y | N | Y | N | Y | N | Y | N | Y | N | Y | N | Y | N | Y | N |
| *TAG "PROMOTIONAL"* | X | X | X | X | X | X | X | X | | | | | | | | |
| *TAG "REGULAR"* | | | | | | | | | X | X | X | X | X | X | X | X |
| *TAG "1 YEAR"* | X | X | X | X | | | | | X | X | X | X | | | | |
| *TAG "2 YEAR"* | | | | | X | X | X | X | | | | | X | X | X | X |
| *TAG "PAID"* | X | X | | | X | X | | | X | X | | | X | X | | |
| *TAG "BILL"* | | | X | X | | | X | X | | | X | X | | | X | X |
| *TAG "BULKMAIL"* | X | | X | | X | | X | | X | | X | | X | | X | |
| *TAG "SINGLE MAIL"* | | X | | X | | X | | X | | X | | X | | X | | X |

*Figure 2.6*

lowed by the remaining "no's." Condition 3 will similarly be broken into groupings of one-eighth the total number of rules; condition 4 will be broken into sixteenths, and so on.

When a table is set up in the above manner the following formulas may be helpful. Where $N$ = number of conditions,

Condition 1 = $\frac{1}{2}$ $(2^N)$ "yes" + $\frac{1}{2}$ $(2^N)$ "no"

Condition 2 = $\frac{1}{4}$ $(2^N)$ "yes" + $\frac{1}{4}$ $(2^N)$ "no" + $\frac{1}{4}$ $(2^N)$ "yes" + $\frac{1}{4}$ $(2^N)$ "no"

Condition 3 = $\frac{1}{8}$ $(2^N)$ "yes" + $\frac{1}{8}$ $(2^N)$ "no" + $\frac{1}{8}$ $(2^N)$ "yes" + $\frac{1}{8}$ $(2^N)$ "no" + $\frac{1}{8}$ $(2^N)$ "yes" + $\frac{1}{8}$ $(2^N)$ "no" + $\frac{1}{8}$ $(2^N)$ "yes" + $\frac{1}{8}$ $(2^N)$ "no"

Condition 4 = $\frac{1}{16}$ $(2^N)$ "yes" + $\frac{1}{16}$ $(2^N)$ "no," etc.

Condition 5 = $\frac{1}{32}$ $(2^N)$ "yes" + $\frac{1}{32}$ $(2^N)$ "no," etc.

When this table is completely filled out a pattern exists not only in the condition entry portion of the table but in the action entry part as well. The systematic filling in of the condition responses results in this pattern in the actions. However, tables that have logical interaction do not necessarily have such action patterns.

In general nothing is to be gained by putting conditions having no logical interaction in the same table. The four conditions used in this problem could have been placed in separate tables if each table contained an action referencing the next table. Figure 2.7 shows such a series of one-line tables. These will accomplish exactly the same result as the one large table.

| DECISION LOGIC TABLE | | | Job *MAGAZINE*   Date<br>Prepared by *MORTON* | | | | | | | | |
|---|---|---|---|---|---|---|---|---|---|---|---|
| TABLE 1 | 1 | 2 | | | | | | | | | |
| PROMOTIONAL ? | Y | N | | | | | | | | | |
| TAG "PROMOTIONAL" | X | | | | | | | | | | |
| TAG "REGULAR" | | X | | | | | | | | | |
| GO TO TABLE 2 | X | X | | | | | | | | | |
| | | | | | | | | | | | |
| TABLE 2 | 1 | 2 | | | | | | | | | |
| FOR ONE YEAR ? | Y | N | | | | | | | | | |
| TAG "1 YEAR" | X | | | | | | | | | | |
| TAG "2 YEARS" | | X | | | | | | | | | |
| GO TO TABLE 3 | X | X | | | | | | | | | |
| | | | | | | | | | | | |
| TABLE 3 | 1 | 2 | | | | | | | | | |
| PAYMENT ENCLOSED ? | Y | N | | | | | | | | | |
| TAG "PAID" | X | | | | | | | | | | |
| TAG "BILL" | | X | | | | | | | | | |
| GO TO TABLE 4 | X | X | | | | | | | | | |
| | | | | | | | | | | | |

*Figure 2.7*

## METHODS OF TESTING

There are two commonly accepted methods of using decision logic tables to process data. In one method the data to be processed are charted as a data rule column to be matched against the actual decision table in order to ascertain which actions are applicable. For example, a subscription order might be received that is not the result of the promotion, is a one-year subscription, with no payment enclosed, and is for city delivery. This can be plotted as a rule in an imaginary table as shown in Figure 2.8. This designed rule is then matched against the actual rules contained in the table until one is found that exactly matches the situation. The match starts with rule 1 and moves to the right until the match is made; hence the number of tests might be as few as one (if the first rule matches) or as many as the total of rules shown (if the last rule matches). In this case rule 11 matches the data, and so the actions indicated for rule 11 are taken. This method of testing is called "testing rule by rule."

The second commonly used method is called "testing condition by condition." By answering one condition at a time you can see some interesting things happen. If the subscription *is not* a promotional, suddenly half of the table is out of consideration

| DECISION LOGIC TABLE | | Job *MAGAZINE*  Date |
|---|---|---|
| | | Prepared by  *MORTON* |
| *DATA FOR AN ORDER* | *DATA* | |
| *PROMOTIONAL ?* | N | |
| *FOR ONE YEAR ?* | Y | |
| *PAYMENT ENCLOSED ?* | N | |
| *FOR CITY DELIVERY ?* | Y | |
| | | |
| | | |

*Figure 2.8*

| DECISION LOGIC TABLE | | Job *MAGAZINE* Date | | | | | | | | | | | | | | |
|---|---|---|---|---|---|---|---|---|---|---|---|---|---|---|---|---|
| | | Prepared by *MORTON* | | | | | | | | | | | | | | |

*SUBSCRIPTIONS*

| | 1 | 2 | 3 | 4 | 5 | 6 | 7 | 8 | 9 | 1φ | 11 | 12 | 13 | 14 | 15 | 16 |
|---|---|---|---|---|---|---|---|---|---|---|---|---|---|---|---|---|
| *PROMOTIONAL ?* | Y | Y | Y | Y | Y | Y | Y | Y | N | N | N | N | N | N | N | N |
| *FOR ONE YEAR ?* | Y | Y | Y | Y | N | N | N | N | Y | Y | Y | Y | N | N | N | N |
| *PAYMENT ENCLOSED ?* | Y | Y | N | N | Y | Y | N | N | Y | Y | N | N | Y | Y | N | N |
| *FOR CITY DELIVERY ?* | Y | N | Y | N | Y | N | Y | N | Y | N | Y | N | Y | N | Y | N |
| *TAG "PROMOTIONAL"* | X | X | X | X | X | X | X | X | | | | | | | | |
| *TAG "REGULAR"* | | | | | | | | | X | X | X | X | X | X | X | X |
| *TAG "1 YEAR"* | X | X | X | X | | | | | X | X | X | X | | | | |
| *TAG "2 YEAR"* | | | | | X | X | X | X | | | | | X | X | X | X |
| *TAG "PAID"* | X | X | | | X | X | | | X | X | | | X | X | | |
| *TAG "BILL"* | | | X | X | | | X | X | | | X | X | | | X | X |
| *TAG "BULKMAIL"* | X | | X | | X | | X | | X | | X | | X | | X | |
| *TAG "SINGLE MAIL"* | | X | | X | | X | | X | | X | | X | | X | | X |

*Figure 2.9*

because the rules in that half contain a "yes" response to "Promotional?" (see Fig. 2.9). Even so, when condition 2 is tested you still have the option of answering it "yes" or "no"; if you did not have this option there would be no reason for testing the condition. If the subscription *is* for one year that part of the table responding "no" to condition 2 will be out of consideration for this particular situation (Fig. 2.10). The option of branching "yes" or "no" in response to condition 3 still exists in the remaining applicable portion of the table. Whichever way condition 3 is answered, half of the remaining table is ruled out. The shaded portion in Figure 2.11 indicates that condition 3 was answered "no" for a particular case.

Even though only two rule columns remain applicable after the three tests made thus far, the option still remains to answer condition 4 ("City delivery?") "yes" or "no." Suppose that this condition is answered "yes"; the applicable actions become apparent in Figure 2.12.

In testing this particular table condition by condition any combination of condition responses can be found with four tests, one for each condition. If the same table were tested rule by rule

| DECISION LOGIC TABLE | | | | | | | | Job *MAGAZINE*  Date Prepared by  *MORTON* | | | | | | | |
|---|---|---|---|---|---|---|---|---|---|---|---|---|---|---|---|
| **SUBSCRIPTIONS** | | | | | | | | | | | | | | | |
| | 1 | 2 | 3 | 4 | 5 | 6 | 7 | 8 | 9 | 10 | 11 | 12 | 13 | 14 | 15 | 16 |
| PROMOTIONAL ? | Y | Y | Y | Y | Y | Y | Y | Y | N | N | N | N | N | N | N | N |
| FOR ONE YEAR ? | Y | Y | Y | Y | N | N | N | N | Y | Y | Y | Y | N | N | N | N |
| PAYMENT ENCLOSED ? | Y | Y | N | N | Y | Y | N | N | Y | Y | N | N | Y | Y | N | N |
| FOR CITY DELIVERY? | Y | N | Y | N | Y | N | Y | N | Y | N | Y | N | Y | N | Y | N |
| TAG "PROMOTIONAL" | X | X | X | X | X | X | X | X | | | | | | | | |
| TAG "REGULAR" | | | | | | | | | X | X | X | X | X | X | X | X |
| TAG "1 YEAR" | X | X | X | X | | | | | X | X | X | X | | | | |
| TAG "2 YEAR" | | | | | X | X | X | X | | | | | X | X | X | X |
| TAG "PAID" | X | X | | | X | X | | | X | X | | | X | X | | |
| TAG "BILL" | | | X | X | | | X | X | | | X | X | | | X | X |
| TAG "BULKMAIL" | X | | X | | X | | X | | X | | X | | X | | X | |
| TAG "SINGLE MAIL" | | X | | X | | X | | X | | X | | X | | X | | X |
| | | | | | | | | | | | | | | | | |
| | | | | | | | | | | | | | | | | |

*Figure 2.10*

the number of tests would range from 1 to 16. Testing the same table rule by rule would have required 11 tests.

The ease of testing condition by condition as compared with testing rule by rule is possible only when the table is in *bifurcated* form. The literal meaning of bifurcated is "two-branched." In other words, in a given path all "yes" responses are grouped together and all "no" responses are grouped together to give the branching option on each test. The primary benefit of bifurcation here is that a response to a test leads unambiguously to the next test or to the appropriate action. Subsequent examples will afford a closer look at bifurcation.

In a bifurcated arrangement each condition tested might be

| DECISION LOGIC TABLE | | Job *MAGAZINE* Date | | | | | | | | | | | | | | |
|---|---|---|---|---|---|---|---|---|---|---|---|---|---|---|---|---|
| | | Prepared by *MORTON* | | | | | | | | | | | | | | |

| SUBSCRIPTIONS | 1 | 2 | 3 | 4 | 5 | 6 | 7 | 8 | 9 | 10 | 11 | 12 | 13 | 14 | 15 | 16 |
|---|---|---|---|---|---|---|---|---|---|---|---|---|---|---|---|---|
| PROMOTIONAL ? | Y | Y | Y | Y | Y | Y | Y | Y | N | N | N | N | N | N | N | N |
| FOR ONE YEAR ? | Y | Y | Y | Y | N | N | N | N | Y | Y | Y | Y | N | N | N | N |
| PAYMENT ENCLOSED ? | Y | Y | N | N | Y | Y | N | N | Y | Y | N | N | Y | Y | N | N |
| FOR CITY DELIVERY ? | Y | N | Y | N | Y | N | Y | N | Y | N | Y | N | Y | N | Y | N |
| TAG "PROMOTIONAL" | X | X | X | X | X | X | X | X | | | | | | | | |
| TAG "REGULAR" | | | | | | | | | X | X | X | X | X | X | X | X |
| TAG "1 YEAR" | X | X | X | X | | | | | X | X | X | X | | | | |
| TAG "2 YEAR" | | | | | X | X | X | X | | | | | X | X | X | X |
| TAG "PAID" | X | X | | | X | X | | | X | X | | | X | X | | |
| TAG "BILL" | | | X | X | | | X | X | | | X | X | | | X | X |
| TAG "BULKMAIL" | X | | X | | X | | X | | X | | X | | X | | X | |
| TAG "SINGLE MAIL" | | X | | X | | X | | X | | X | | X | | X | | X |
| | | | | | | | | | | | | | | | | |
| | | | | | | | | | | | | | | | | |
| | | | | | | | | | | | | | | | | |

*Figure 2.11*

compared with a test block in a two-branch flowchart: you may answer "yes" or "no," and each path leads either to a subsequent test or to an action to be performed. A simple two-branch flowchart for the magazine-subscription problem is shown in Figure 2.13. Each condition from the table is shown in a decision block; each action is shown in an action box.

## CONVERTING A FLOWCHART TO A DECISION TABLE

It was stated earlier that flowcharts and decision tables are alternative methods of structuring the logic of a problem segment. For proof of this statement, convert the flowchart shown in Figure 2.14 into a limited-entry decision logic table.

| DECISION LOGIC TABLE | | Job *MAGAZINE* Date | | | | | | | | | | | | | | |
|---|---|---|---|---|---|---|---|---|---|---|---|---|---|---|---|---|
| | | Prepared by *MORTON* | | | | | | | | | | | | | | |

| SUBSCRIPTIONS | 1 | 2 | 3 | 4 | 5 | 6 | 7 | 8 | 9 | 10 | 11 | 12 | 13 | 14 | 15 | 16 |
|---|---|---|---|---|---|---|---|---|---|---|---|---|---|---|---|---|
| PROMOTIONAL ? | Y | Y | Y | Y | Y | Y | Y | Y | N | N | N | N | N | N | N | N |
| FOR ONE YEAR ? | Y | Y | Y | Y | N | N | N | N | Y | Y | Y | Y | N | N | N | N |
| PAYMENT ENCLOSED? | Y | Y | N | N | Y | Y | N | N | Y | Y | N | N | Y | Y | N | N |
| FOR CITY DELIVERY ? | Y | N | Y | N | Y | N | Y | N | Y | N | Y | N | Y | N | Y | N |
| TAG "PROMOTIONAL" | X | X | X | X | X | X | X | X | | | | | | | | |
| TAG "REGULAR" | | | | | | | | | X | X | X | X | X | X | X | X |
| TAG " 1 YEAR" | X | X | X | X | | | | | X | X | X | X | | | | |
| TAG "2 YEAR" | | | | | X | X | X | X | | | | | X | X | X | X |
| TAG "PAID" | X | X | | | X | X | | | X | X | | | X | X | | |
| TAG "BILL" | | | X | X | | | X | X | | | X | X | | | X | X |
| TAG "BULKMAIL" | X | | X | | X | | X | | X | | X | | X | | X | |
| TAG "SINGLE MAIL" | | X | | X | | X | | X | | X | | X | | X | | X |
| | | | | | | | | | | | | | | | | |
| | | | | | | | | | | | | | | | | |

*Figure 2.12*

It is obvious from the flowchart that there are five conditions and four actions. Start with a table similar to that shown in Figure 2.15. Probably the easiest way of establishing all the rules shown is to start at an action box and trace backward to condition 1. For example, trace back from the action box indicating action 3 on the right side of the chart. In any rule column on the table place "X" by action 3. Then in the same rule column indicate that the answer to condition 5 is "yes"; condition 4 is "yes"; condition 3 is "yes"; condition 2 is "no"; condition 1 is "yes." Figure 2.16 shows this rule. One rule is equal to one path on the flowchart.

To avoid duplicating a path it is a good idea to place a check

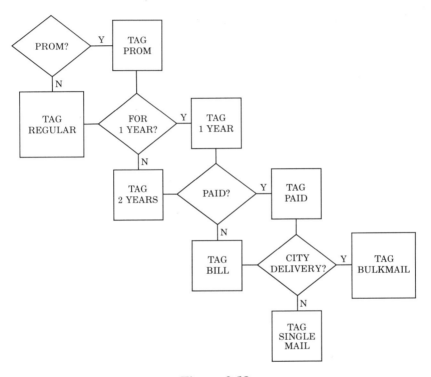

*Figure 2.13*

mark by the action box on the flowchart. When you have completed this conversion from flowchart to decision table form you should have 10 rules (10 action boxes are shown on the flowchart).

If you have successfully converted the flowchart your decision table should contain the same 10 rules shown in Figure 2.17, but

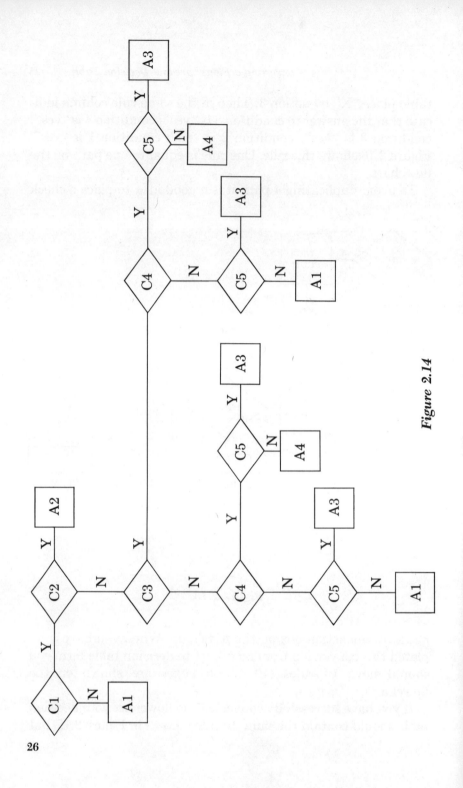

Figure 2.14

26

| DECISION LOGIC TABLE | Job *CONVERSION* Date *4-27-66* Prepared by *MASON* | | | | | | | | | | |
|---|---|---|---|---|---|---|---|---|---|---|---|
| *FLOWCHART TO DLT* | | | | | | | | | | | |
| *CONDITION 1 ?* | | | | | | | | | | | |
| *CONDITION 2 ?* | | | | | | | | | | | |
| *CONDITION 3 ?* | | | | | | | | | | | |
| *CONDITION 4 ?* | | | | | | | | | | | |
| *CONDITION 5 ?* | | | | | | | | | | | |
| *ACTION 1* | | | | | | | | | | | |
| *ACTION 2* | | | | | | | | | | | |
| *ACTION 3* | | | | | | | | | | | |
| *ACTION 4* | | | | | | | | | | | |
| | | | | | | | | | | | |
| | | | | | | | | | | | |

*Figure 2.15*

| DECISION LOGIC TABLE | Job *CONVERSION* Date *4-27-66* Prepared by *MASON* | | | | | | | | | |
|---|---|---|---|---|---|---|---|---|---|---|
| *FLOWCHART TO DLT* | | | | | | | | | | |
| *CONDITION 1 ?* | *Y* | | | | | | | | | |
| *CONDITION 2 ?* | *N* | | | | | | | | | |
| *CONDITION 3 ?* | *Y* | | | | | | | | | |
| *CONDITION 4 ?* | *Y* | | | | | | | | | |
| *CONDITION 5 ?* | *Y* | | | | | | | | | |
| *ACTION 1* | | | | | | | | | | |
| *ACTION 2* | | | | | | | | | | |
| *ACTION 3* | *X* | | | | | | | | | |
| *ACTION 4* | | | | | | | | | | |
| | | | | | | | | | | |
| | | | | | | | | | | |

*Figure 2.16*

| DECISION LOGIC TABLE | | Job *CONVERSION* Date *4-27-66* |
|---|---|---|
| | | Prepared by *MASON* |

*FLOWCHART TO DLT*

| | 1 | 2 | 3 | 4 | 5 | 6 | 7 | 8 | 9 | 10 |
|---|---|---|---|---|---|---|---|---|---|---|
| CONDITION 1 ? | N | Y | Y | Y | Y | Y | Y | Y | Y | Y |
| CONDITION 2 ? | | N | N | N | N | N | N | N | N | Y |
| CONDITION 3 ? | | N | N | N | N | Y | Y | Y | Y | |
| CONDITION 4 ? | | N | N | Y | Y | N | N | Y | Y | |
| CONDITION 5 ? | | N | Y | N | Y | N | Y | N | Y | |
| ACTION 1 | X | X | | | | X | | | | |
| ACTION 2 | | | | | | | | | | X |
| ACTION 3 | | | X | | X | | X | | X | |
| ACTION 4 | | | | X | | | | X | | |
| | | | | | | | | | | |
| | | | | | | | | | | |

*Figure 2.17*

not necessarily in the same order. Whether the rule that says, "If condition 1 is 'no,' then do action 1," is numbered rule 1 or rule 10 makes no difference as long as you have represented all 10 rules.

Examine the table shown in Figure 2.17. Can it be simplified? Rules 3 and 5 both result in the same action (3), and their only difference is in their responses to condition 4; obviously condition 4 is irrelevant in these two paths. These two can be combined into a single rule, leaving a blank by condition 4 in a new table (Fig. 2.18).

Of the rules remaining (Fig. 2.19) rules 4 and 8 are exactly alike except in their responses to condition 3. Since they result in the same action they can also be combined and carried to a new table. Also note that rules 7 and 9 are identical except in their responses to condition 4. They can be combined and moved to the new table. Rules 2 and 6 are alike except for their

| DECISION LOGIC TABLE | Job *CONVERSION* Date *4-27-66* <br> Prepared by *MASON* |
|---|---|

*FLOWCHART TO DLT*

*3-5*

| | | | | | | | | | | |
|---|---|---|---|---|---|---|---|---|---|---|
| CONDITION 1 ? | Y | | | | | | | | | |
| CONDITION 2 ? | N | | | | | | | | | |
| CONDITION 3 ? | N | | | | | | | | | |
| CONDITION 4 ? | | | | | | | | | | |
| CONDITION 5 ? | Y | | | | | | | | | |
| ACTION 1 | | | | | | | | | | |
| ACTION 2 | | | | | | | | | | |
| ACTION 3 | X | | | | | | | | | |
| ACTION 4 | | | | | | | | | | |
| | | | | | | | | | | |
| | | | | | | | | | | |

**Figure 2.18**

| DECISION LOGIC TABLE | Job *CONVERSION* Date *4-27-66* <br> Prepared by *MASON* |
|---|---|

*FLOWCHART TO DLT*

| | 1 | 2 | 3 | 4 | 5 | 6 | 7 | 8 | 9 | 10 |
|---|---|---|---|---|---|---|---|---|---|---|
| CONDITION 1 ? | N | Y | Y | Y | Y | Y | Y | Y | Y | Y |
| CONDITION 2 ? | | N | N | N | N | N | N | N | N | Y |
| CONDITION 3 ? | | N | N | N | Y | Y | Y | Y | | |
| CONDITION 4 ? | | N | N | Y | Y | N | N | Y | Y | |
| CONDITION 5 ? | | N | Y | N | Y | N | Y | N | Y | |
| ACTION 1 | X | X | | | | X | | | | |
| ACTION 2 | | | | | | | | | | X |
| ACTION 3 | | | X | | X | | X | | X | |
| ACTION 4 | | | | X | | | | X | | |
| | | | | | | | | | | |
| | | | | | | | | | | |

**Figure 2.19**

responses to condition 3. They too can be combined and moved to the new table.

Notice that the table in Figure 2.20 has only two rules remaining: rules 1 and 10. These cannot be combined but must be carried as they are to the new table if the new table is to reflect all relevant information contained in the original. Figure 2.21 shows the new table with the combinations accomplished and rules 1

| DECISION LOGIC TABLE | | Job *CONVERSION* Date *4-27-66*<br>Prepared by *MASON* | | | | | | | | | |
|---|---|---|---|---|---|---|---|---|---|---|---|
| *FLOWCHART TO DLT* | | | | | | | | | | | |
| | | 1 | 2 | 3 | 4 | 5 | 6 | 7 | 8 | 9 | 10 |
| CONDITION 1 ? | | N | Y | Y | Y | Y | Y | Y | Y | Y | Y |
| CONDITION 2 ? | | | N | N | N | N | N | N | N | N | Y |
| CONDITION 3 ? | | | N | N | N | N | Y | Y | Y | Y | |
| CONDITION 4 ? | | | N | N | Y | Y | N | N | Y | Y | |
| CONDITION 5 ? | | | N | Y | N | Y | N | Y | N | Y | |
| ACTION 1 | | X | X | | | | X | | | | |
| ACTION 2 | | | | | | | | | | | X |
| ACTION 3 | | | | X | | X | | X | | X | |
| ACTION 4 | | | | | X | | | | X | | |
| | | | | | | | | | | | |
| | | | | | | | | | | | |

*Figure 2.20*

and 10 brought forward unchanged. Are further combinations possible from this table? Rules 3–5 and 7–9 in this table result in the same action, and their only difference is in response to condition 3. They can be combined and moved to a new table (four rules from the original table have now been combined into a single rule). No further combinations are possible in this table, and so all rules remaining should also be copied into the new table. Now look at the table shown in Figure 2.22. There are no responses shown for condition 3, pointing up the fact that it was an irrelevant test in every situation.

Although the table is not now in bifurcated form, it can be put into such form. The table can be rearranged in any fashion as long as you do not change the responses ("yes" or "no") to any condition within a rule *and* as long as the path for each rule con-

| DECISION LOGIC TABLE | Job *CONVERSION* Date *4-27-66* Prepared by *MASON* | | | | | | | | | |
|---|---|---|---|---|---|---|---|---|---|---|
| *FLOWCHART TO DLT* | *3-5* | *4-8* | *7-9* | *2-6* | *1* | *10* | | | | |
| *CONDITION 1 ?* | *Y* | *Y* | *Y* | *Y* | *N* | *Y* | | | | |
| *CONDITION 2 ?* | *N* | *N* | *N* | *N* | | *Y* | | | | |
| *CONDITION 3 ?* | *N* | | *Y* | | | | | | | |
| *CONDITION 4 ?* | | *Y* | | *N* | | | | | | |
| *CONDITION 5 ?* | *Y* | *N* | *Y* | *N* | | | | | | |
| *ACTION 1* | | | | *X* | *X* | | | | | |
| *ACTION 2* | | | | | | *X* | | | | |
| *ACTION 3* | *X* | | *X* | | | | | | | |
| *ACTION 4* | | *X* | | | | | | | | |
| | | | | | | | | | | |
| | | | | | | | | | | |
| | | | | | | | | | | |

*Figure 2.21*

tinues to result in the same action. In a bifurcated table the first condition must have all "yes" responses grouped together and all "no" responses grouped together, with no blanks between the first and last rules. Each following condition must have similar groupings *in a given path* to afford the branching capability; each path has "yes" responses grouped together and "no" responses grouped together as if it were the first line of a new table.

| DECISION LOGIC TABLE | | Job *CONVERSION* Date *4-27-66* |
|---|---|---|
| | | Prepared by *MASON* |

| FLOWCHART TO DLT | 3-5 7-9 | 4-8 | 2-6 | I | 10 | | | | | |
|---|---|---|---|---|---|---|---|---|---|---|
| CONDITION 1 ? | Y | Y | Y | N | Y | | | | | |
| CONDITION 2 ? | N | N | N | | Y | | | | | |
| CONDITION 3 ? | | | | | | | | | | |
| CONDITION 4 ? | | Y | N | | | | | | | |
| CONDITION 5 ? | Y | N | N | | | | | | | |
| ACTION 1 | | X | X | | | | | | | |
| ACTION 2 | | | X | | | | | | | |
| ACTION 3 | X | | | | | | | | | |
| ACTION 4 | | X | | | | | | | | |
| | | | | | | | | | | |
| | | | | | | | | | | |
| | | | | | | | | | | |

*Figure 2.22*

Since blanks are not permitted in a path, the sequence of conditions will have to be changed. The condition having the greatest number of responses must appear first in the table. In this case condition 1 has the most responses; therefore leave it first. The condition having the second greatest number of conditions must be second in the table and so condition 2 will remain second. Condition 5 has more responses than does condition 4, and so condition 5 will appear above 4 in the new table. Figure 2.23 shows the shifted conditions with their responses.

Now the rules must be rearranged in order to put the table into bifurcated form. By switching the position of rules 1 and 10 as shown in Figure 2.24, groupings of responses are achieved and the table is bifurcated. Try testing it condition by condition to be certain.

Figure 2.25 shows the same table in a different arrangement, but also in bifurcated form. There are several such arrangements possible for a table. The only sure way to check bifurcation is to test it carefully, condition by condition, yourself.

| DECISION LOGIC TABLE | Job *CONVERSION*  Date *4-27-66* |
| --- | --- |
|  | Prepared by  *MASON* |

FLOWCHART TO DLT

| | 3-5 7-9 | 4-8 | 2-6 | 1 | 10 | | | | | |
| --- | --- | --- | --- | --- | --- | --- | --- | --- | --- | --- |
| CONDITION 1 ? | Y | Y | Y | N | Y | | | | | |
| CONDITION 2 ? | N | N | N |  | Y | | | | | |
| CONDITION 5 ? | Y | N | N | | | | | | | |
| CONDITION 4 ? | | Y | N | | | | | | | |
| ACTION 1 | | | X | X | | | | | | |
| ACTION 2 | | | | X | | | | | | |
| ACTION 3 | X | | | | | | | | | |
| ACTION 4 | | X | | | | | | | | |
| | | | | | | | | | | |
| | | | | | | | | | | |
| | | | | | | | | | | |

**Figure 2.23**

| DECISION LOGIC TABLE | Job *CONVERSION* Date *4-27-66* |
| --- | --- |
|  | Prepared by  *MASON* |

FLOWCHART TO DLT

| | 3-5 7-9 | 4-8 | 2-6 | 10 | 1 | | | | | |
| --- | --- | --- | --- | --- | --- | --- | --- | --- | --- | --- |
| CONDITION 1 ? | Y | Y | Y | Y | N | | | | | |
| CONDITION 2 ? | N | N | N | Y | | | | | | |
| CONDITION 5 ? | Y | N | N | | | | | | | |
| CONDITION 4 ? | | Y | N | | | | | | | |
| ACTION 1 | | | X | | X | | | | | |
| ACTION 2 | | | | X | | | | | | |
| ACTION 3 | X | | | | | | | | | |
| ACTION 4 | | X | | | | | | | | |
| | | | | | | | | | | |
| | | | | | | | | | | |
| | | | | | | | | | | |

**Figure 2.24**

33

| DECISION LOGIC TABLE | | Job *CONVERSION*  Date *4-27-66* | | | | | | | | |
|---|---|---|---|---|---|---|---|---|---|---|
| | | Prepared by  *MASON* | | | | | | | | |

*FLOWCHART TO DLT*

| | 1 | 10 | 3-5 7-9 | 4-8 | 2-6 | | | | | |
|---|---|---|---|---|---|---|---|---|---|---|
| CONDITION 1 ? | N | Y | Y | Y | Y | | | | | |
| CONDITION 2 ? | | Y | N | N | N | | | | | |
| CONDITION 5 ? | | | Y | N | N | | | | | |
| CONDITION 4 ? | | | | Y | N | | | | | |
| ACTION 1 | X | | | X | | | | | | |
| ACTION 2 | | X | | | | | | | | |
| ACTION 3 | | | X | | | | | | | |
| ACTION 4 | | | | X | | | | | | |
| | | | | | | | | | | |
| | | | | | | | | | | |
| | | | | | | | | | | |

**Figure 2.25**

If a table connot be arranged in bifurcated form, chances are that it contains contradictions, redundancies, or omissions. In a truly bifurcated table containing $2^N$ rules, the rules in combination are exhaustive and mutually exclusive. An important exception to this is a table containing an ELSE rule. The ELSE rule, by definition, includes all rules not specifically covered in the table.

Usually the ELSE rule is merely a catch-all rule placed at the extreme right of the table with a special symbol in the rule header that identifies it as such. Often the rule is nothing more than a rule column with blanks shown as response to all conditions and an appropriate action indicated by an "X" in the action entry portion of the table. Such an arrangement is especially desirable in working with unedited data, because it detects "illegal" codes. The usage varies from installation to installation and from table processor to table processor.

## CONVERTING A SIMPLIFIED DECISION LOGIC TABLE
## TO A TWO-BRANCH FLOWCHART

Now convert the simplified decision table (Figure 2.24) to a simple two-branch flowchart. Place each condition in a test block and each action in an action box. Check your finished flowchart against that shown in Figure 2.26. This flowchart contains all essential processing steps of the original, much larger table with which we started (Fig. 2.14). Through the use of decision logic tables the superfluous tests have been removed and the problem has been greatly reduced and simplified.

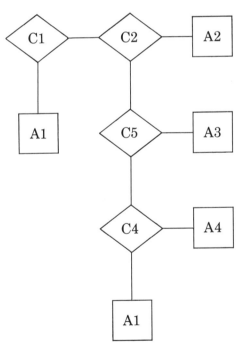

*Figure 2.26*

## SIMPLICATION THROUGH VISUAL INSPECTION

Figure 2.27 shows highly stylized characters that one banking firm uses as account numbers on checks. Is is possible to acertain the identity of a character by making the tests shown in the decision table in Figure 2.28; but surely some superfluous tests are being made. Since no two rules result in the same action we cannot combine any two rules as before. But in such cases, when the tables are to be used extensively, it is worth the effort to inspect visually and simplify the table.

Note that rule 1 (which results in "Number is 0") and rule 9 (which results in "Number is 8") are the only two rules that answer both condition 1 and condition 2 "yes," Even though they are identical thus far, they are *different* from all other rules in our table. Rules 1 and 9 both also answer condition 3 as "yes." But notice that in response to condition 4 rule 1 has "no" and rule 9 has "yes." This is the first *difference* in the two rules. At this point (after testing condition 4) rule 1 contains a combination of responses different from all other rules in the table; rule 9 also is unique with respect to all other rules in the table. Hence it is not necessary to test condition 5 for either of these rules, and so the response area for condition 5 should be left blank in both paths.

Now notice that rules 3 and 6 (Figure 2.29) are the only two in the table that have a "no" response to both condition 1 and 2. The response to condition 3 is "yes" for both rules, but in response to condition 4 rule 3 has "no" and rule 6 has "yes." The response to condition 4 makes each of these a unique combination within the table. Again it is unnecessary to test condition 5 for either of these rules. Rule 7 in the table becomes unique after testing condition 2; no further tests are required to

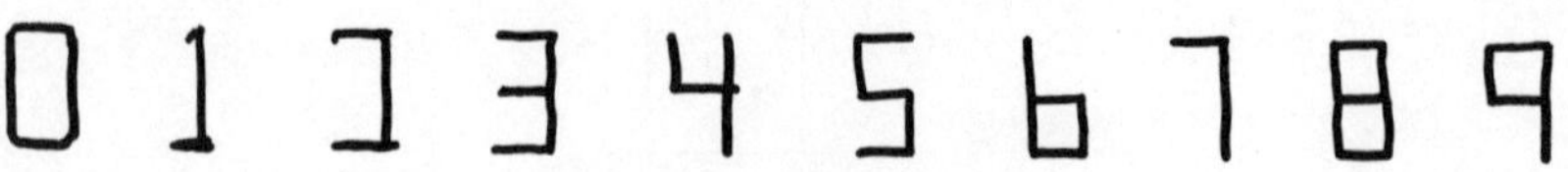

*Figure 2.27*

| DECISION LOGIC TABLE | Job *CHECKING ACCT.* Date *3-20-65* <br> Prepared by   *RICE* | | | | | | | | | |
|---|---|---|---|---|---|---|---|---|---|---|
| *RECOGNITION* | *1* | *2* | *3* | *4* | *5* | *6* | *7* | *8* | *9* | *10* |
| *LONG VERTICAL LEFT ?* | Y | N | N | N | N | N | Y | N | Y | N |
| *LONG VERTICAL RIGHT ?* | Y | Y | N | Y | Y | N | N | Y | Y | Y |
| *HORIZONTAL  TOP ?* | Y | N | Y | Y | N | Y | N | Y | Y | Y |
| *HORIZONTAL  MIDDLE ?* | N | N | N | Y | Y | Y | Y | N | Y | Y |
| *HORIZONTAL  BOTTOM ?* | Y | Y | Y | Y | N | Y | Y | N | Y | N |
| *NUMBER IS  ∅* | X | | | | | | | | | |
| *NUMBER IS  1* | | X | | | | | | | | |
| *NUMBER IS  2* | | | X | | | | | | | |
| *NUMBER IS  3* | | | | X | | | | | | |
| *NUMBER IS  4* | | | | | X | | | | | |
| *NUMBER IS  5* | | | | | | X | | | | |
| *NUMBER IS  6* | | | | | | | X | | | |
| *NUMBER IS  7* | | | | | | | | X | | |
| *NUMBER IS  8* | | | | | | | | | X | |
| *NUMBER IS  9* | | | | | | | | | | X |
| | | | | | | | | | | |
| | | | | | | | | | | |

*Figure 2.28*

identify the number as a 6. Rules 2 and 5 are identical in their responses until condition 4 is tested. Rule 2 answers condition 4 as "no"; rule 5 answers "yes." There is no need to test condition 5 for either of these paths. The responses of the three remaining rules (rules 4, 8, and 10) are identical until condition 4 is tested. Rules 4 and 10 both answer "yes"; rule 8 answers "no." Thus rule 8 becomes different from all other rules in the table and further testing is not necessary. However, rules 4 and 10 are still identical, indicating that further testing is required to identify the number. When condition 5 is tested rule 4 has a response of "yes" and rule 10 has a response of "no." Consequently rules 4 and 10 are the only ones requiring testing of all five conditions.

Figure 2.30 shows the table with the above changes indicated. By changing the positions of condition 4 ("Horizontal middle?")

| DECISION LOGIC TABLE | Job *CHECKING ACCT.* Date *3-20-65* Prepared by *RICE* | | | | | | | | | |
|---|---|---|---|---|---|---|---|---|---|---|
| *RECOGNITION* | 1 | 2 | 3 | 4 | 5 | 6 | 7 | 8 | 9 | 10 |
| *LONG VERTICAL LEFT ?* | Y | N | N | N | N | N | Y | N | Y | N |
| *LONG VERTICAL RIGHT ?* | Y | Y | N | Y | Y | N | N | Y | Y | Y |
| *HORIZONTAL TOP ?* | Y | N | Y | Y | N | Y | N | Y | Y | Y |
| *HORIZONTAL MIDDLE ?* | N | N | N | Y | Y | Y | Y | N | Y | Y |
| *HORIZONTAL BOTTOM ?* | Y | Y | Y | Y | N | Y | Y | N | Y | N |
| *NUMBER IS 0* | X | | | | | | | | | |
| *NUMBER IS 1* | | X | | | | | | | | |
| *NUMBER IS 2* | | | X | | | | | | | |
| *NUMBER IS 3* | | | | X | | | | | | |
| *NUMBER IS 4* | | | | | X | | | | | |
| *NUMBER IS 5* | | | | | | X | | | | |
| *NUMBER IS 6* | | | | | | | X | | | |
| *NUMBER IS 7* | | | | | | | | X | | |
| *NUMBER IS 8* | | | | | | | | | X | |
| *NUMBER IS 9* | | | | | | | | | | X |
| | | | | | | | | | | |
| | | | | | | | | | | |
| | | | | | | | | | | |

*Figure 2.29*

and condition 3 ("Horizontal top?") in this table, some further tests can be eliminated. Figure 2.31 shows the condition shifted. Note that in the new form rules 1 and 9 both become unique on testing for "Horizontal middle?" Their response is "yes" to the "Horizontal top?" in each instance, and so that test need not be made. Rules 3 and 6 also become unique when the test for "Horizontal middle?" is made. Since they both respond "yes" to the remaining condition, that test is not necessary; the identity of the numbers has already been established.

In this particular table no benefit is derived from placing

| DECISION LOGIC TABLE | | Job *CHECKING ACCT.* Date *3-20-65* Prepared by *RICE* | | | | | | | | |
|---|---|---|---|---|---|---|---|---|---|---|
| RECOGNITION | | | | | | | | | | |
| | 1 | 2 | 3 | 4 | 5 | 6 | 7 | 8 | 9 | 10 |
| LONG VERTICAL LEFT ? | Y | N | N | N | N | N | Y | N | Y | N |
| LONG VERTICAL RIGHT ? | Y | Y | N | Y | Y | N | N | Y | Y | Y |
| HORIZONTAL TOP ? | Y | N | Y | Y | N | Y | | Y | Y | Y |
| HORIZONTAL MIDDLE ? | N | N | N | Y | Y | Y | | N | Y | Y |
| HORIZONTAL BOTTOM ? | | | | Y | | | | | | N |
| NUMBER IS Ø | X | | | | | | | | | |
| NUMBER IS 1 | | X | | | | | | | | |
| NUMBER IS 2 | | | X | | | | | | | |
| NUMBER IS 3 | | | | X | | | | | | |
| NUMBER IS 4 | | | | | X | | | | | |
| NUMBER IS 5 | | | | | | X | | | | |
| NUMBER IS 6 | | | | | | | X | | | |
| NUMBER IS 7 | | | | | | | | X | | |
| NUMBER IS 8 | | | | | | | | | X | |
| NUMBER IS 9 | | | | | | | | | | X |

*Figure 2.30*

condition 2 before condition 1; all responses to both conditions are still required in order to identify the character.

Superfluous tests appear to have been eliminated in the table, as shown in Figure 2.32. But as it stands the table cannot be tested condition by condition. The table can be bifurcated, which is a good indication that superfluous tests have been eliminated. One version of the table in bifurcated form is shown in Figure 2.33. It is possible to test this table condition by condition. Thus the numeral 6 can be identified in only two tests; only

| DECISION LOGIC TABLE | | Job *CHECKING ACCT.* Date *3-20-65*  Prepared by *RICE* | | | | | | | | |
|---|---|---|---|---|---|---|---|---|---|---|
| *RECOGNITION* | 1 | 2 | 3 | 4 | 5 | 6 | 7 | 8 | 9 | 10 |
| *LONG VERTICAL LEFT ?* | Y | N | N | N | N | N | Y | N | Y | N |
| *LONG VERTICAL RIGHT ?* | Y | Y | N | Y | Y | N | N | Y | Y | Y |
| *HORIZONTAL MIDDLE ?* | N | N | N | Y | Y | Y | | N | Y | Y |
| *HORIZONTAL TOP ?* | Y | N | Y | Y | N | Y | | Y | Y | Y |
| *HORIZONTAL BOTTOM ?* | | | | Y | | | | | | N |
| *NUMBER IS 0* | X | | | | | | | | | |
| *NUMBER IS 1* | | X | | | | | | | | |
| *NUMBER IS 2* | | | X | | | | | | | |
| *NUMBER IS 3* | | | | X | | | | | | |
| *NUMBER IS 4* | | | | | X | | | | | |
| *NUMBER IS 5* | | | | | | X | | | | |
| *NUMBER IS 6* | | | | | | | X | | | |
| *NUMBER IS 7* | | | | | | | | X | | |
| *NUMBER IS 8* | | | | | | | | | X | |
| *NUMBER IS 9* | | | | | | | | | | X |

*Figure 2.31*

three tests are required to identify the numbers 8, 0, 5, and 2. On the fourth test it is possible to distinguish the numbers 7, 1, and 4. All five tests are required to identify only the numbers 9 and 3.

As a result of visual inspection and removing unnecessary tests, the table may now be tested condition by condition. With the table in its present form it is possible to make a minimum of two and a maximum of five tests to identify any number. In its

| DECISION LOGIC TABLE | Job *CHECKING ACCT.* Date *3-20-65* Prepared by *RICE* | | | | | | | | | |
|---|---|---|---|---|---|---|---|---|---|---|
| *RECOGNITION* | *1* | *2* | *3* | *4* | *5* | *6* | *7* | *8* | *9* | *10* |
| *LONG VERTICAL LEFT ?* | Y | N | N | N | N | N | Y | N | Y | N |
| *LONG VERTICAL RIGHT ?* | Y | Y | N | Y | Y | N | N | Y | Y | Y |
| *HORIZONTAL MIDDLE ?* | N | N | N | Y | Y | Y | | N | Y | Y |
| *HORIZONTAL TOP ?* | | N | | Y | N | | | Y | | Y |
| *HORIZONTAL BOTTOM ?* | | | | Y | | | | | | N |
| *NUMBER IS 0* | X | | | | | | | | | |
| *NUMBER IS 1* | | X | | | | | | | | |
| *NUMBER IS 2* | | | X | | | | | | | |
| *NUMBER IS 3* | | | | X | | | | | | |
| *NUMBER IS 4* | | | | | X | | | | | |
| *NUMBER IS 5* | | | | | | X | | | | |
| *NUMBER IS 6* | | | | | | | X | | | |
| *NUMBER IS 7* | | | | | | | | X | | |
| *NUMBER IS 8* | | | | | | | | | X | |
| *NUMBER IS 9* | | | | | | | | | | X |
| | | | | | | | | | | |
| | | | | | | | | | | |
| | | | | | | | | | | |

*Figure 2.32*

original form Fig. 2.28) the table had to be tested rule by rule and involved a minimum of one test, a maximum of 10.

The saving of test time is enormous when you consider the millions of checks that will be processed each week using these

| DECISION LOGIC TABLE | | | | Job *CHECKING ACCT.* Date *3-20-65*  Prepared by *RICE* | | | | | | |
|---|---|---|---|---|---|---|---|---|---|---|
| **RECOGNITION** | 7 | 9 | 1 | 8 | 2 | 5 | 10 | 4 | 6 | 3 |
| LONG VERTICAL LEFT ? | Y | Y | Y | N | N | N | N | N | N | N |
| LONG VERTICAL RIGHT ? | N | Y | Y | Y | Y | Y | Y | Y | N | N |
| HORIZONTAL MIDDLE ? |  | Y | N | N | N | Y | Y | Y | Y | N |
| HORIZONTAL TOP ? |  |  |  | Y | N | N | Y | Y |  |  |
| HORIZONTAL BOTTOM ? |  |  |  |  |  |  | N | Y |  |  |
| NUMBER IS 0 |  |  |  | X |  |  |  |  |  |  |
| NUMBER IS 1 |  |  |  |  | X |  |  |  |  |  |
| NUMBER IS 2 |  |  |  |  |  |  |  |  |  | X |
| NUMBER IS 3 |  |  |  |  |  |  |  | X |  |  |
| NUMBER IS 4 |  |  |  |  |  | X |  |  |  |  |
| NUMBER IS 5 |  |  |  |  |  |  |  |  | X |  |
| NUMBER IS 6 | X |  |  |  |  |  |  |  |  |  |
| NUMBER IS 7 |  |  | X |  |  |  |  |  |  |  |
| NUMBER IS 8 |  | X |  |  |  |  |  |  |  |  |
| NUMBER IS 9 |  |  |  |  |  |  | X |  |  |  |
|  |  |  |  |  |  |  |  |  |  |  |
|  |  |  |  |  |  |  |  |  |  |  |
|  |  |  |  |  |  |  |  |  |  |  |

*Figure 2.33*

identification criteria. Any time you are confronted with a table that does not seem to have any possibilities for simplication under any other system, it should be visually inspected for unnecessary tests. The results, as in this case, are often suprising.

# 3

---

# Machine Processing
# of Decision Tables

## GENERAL PROCEDURE

Although many programmers still code by hand directly from completed tables, computer processing of the tables is now a reality. The processing steps vary, depending on which processor is used, but essentially the major steps are similar to those shown in Figure 3.1.

The programmer codes as usual those segments of the program not covered by decision logic tables. He indicates in his coding which tables are to be inserted and exactly where in the program they are to be placed. Each of the actual lines of coding is prefaced by a special symbol to indicate to the table processor that the line is to be passed through the processor unchanged. The tables themselves will result in additional coding being generated and inserted in the program.

In most situations the coding and the tables are punched into cards and the information from the cards is placed on magnetic tape. The table-processor program is read into the computer, followed by the tape containing the program and decision tables

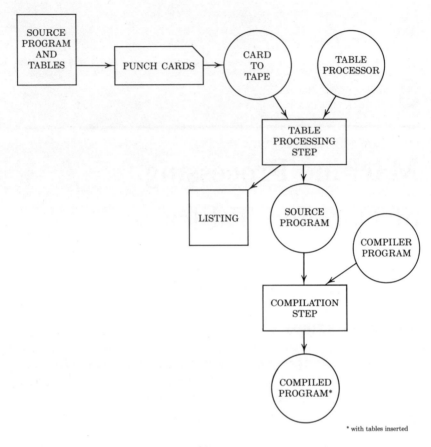

*Figure 3.1*

to be processed. Two outputs result from this operation: (a) a listing of the coding (so that the programmer can verify that the tables were inserted correctly) and (b) a magnetic tape to be used as input to the compilation of the program. This magnetic tape contains the coding written by the programmer and the coding resulting from the processing of the tables.

Inputs to the compilation are the output tape from the table processor and the compiler program. When the results of the compilation are printed (compilation listing) it is often difficult to ascertain whether certain areas were coded by hand or resulted form the processing of the decision tables.

## DECISION TABLES TO FORTRAN

Figure 3.2 shows one of the original tables used in a recode program. Figure 3.3 shows the output listing from the table-processing step. Finally, Figure 3.4 shows the results of the compilation listing. Notice that each test is followed by a GO TO instruction, transferring control to the end of the table; this is to restart the table for each new piece of data.

An example that has logical interaction is shown in Figures 3.5 through 3.7. Note that the processor sets up the negative tests and uses the failure of each test as a "yes" response path.

| DECISION LOGIC TABLE | | Job *RECODE*   Date *5-22-66* | | | | | | | | |
|---|---|---|---|---|---|---|---|---|---|---|
| | | Prepared by *HEAD* | | | | | | | | |
| *SEX CODE* | | | | | | | | | | |
| | | *1* | *2* | | | | | | | |
| *SEX EQUAL ∅ ?* | | Y | N | | | | | | | |
| *SEX CODE = 1* | | X | | | | | | | | |
| *SEX CODE = 2* | | | X | | | | | | | |
| | | | | | | | | | | |
| | | | | | | | | | | |

*Figure 3.2*

```
IB               R.      R.
T    SEX. EQ. 0  . T     . F
A    SEX =        1       2
```

*Figure 3.3*

IF (.NOT. (SEX .EQ. 0)) Go To 224
SEX = 1
GO TO 325
224  SEX = 2
325  CONTINUE

*Figure 3.4*

| DECISION LOGIC TABLE | | Job *RECODE*   Date *2-7-66*<br>Prepared by *BROCK* | | | | | | | | |
|---|---|---|---|---|---|---|---|---|---|---|
| *NTYPE* | | | | | | | | | | |
| | | *1* | *2* | *3* | *4* | | | | | |
| *NTYPE EQUAL NP ?* | | *Y* | *N* | *N* | *N* | | | | | |
| *NTYPE EQUAL NF ?* | | | *Y* | *N* | *N* | | | | | |
| *NTYPE EQUAL NO ?* | | | | *Y* | *N* | | | | | |
| *GO TO 103* | | *X* | *X* | *X* | | | | | | |
| *GO TO 801* | | | | | *X* | | | | | |
| | | | | | | | | | | |
| | | | | | | | | | | |
| | | | | | | | | | | |

*Figure 3.5*

IB

| | | R | R | R | R |
|---|---|---|---|---|---|
| T | NTYPE EQ NP | .T | .F | .F | .F |
| T | NTYPE EQ NF | .. | .T | .F | .F |
| T | NTYPE EQ NO | .. | .. | .T | .T |
| A | GO TO | 103 | 103 | 103 | 801 |

*Figure 3.6*

```
    IF (.NOT. (NTYPE .EQ. NP)) Go To 202
    GO TO    103
    GO TO    505
303 IF (.NOT. (NTYPE .EQ. NO)) Go To 404
    GO TO    103
    GO TO    505
404 GO TO    801
505 CONTINUE
```

*Figure 3.7*

## DEVELOPMENT OF THE FIRST PROCESSOR

In the mid-1950s General Electric's Manufacturing Services Department began experimental work with decision logic tables. Under their early system information was punched into cards in decision table format and the cards were used as input to a computer. Soon the area of usage was expanded until a compiler system was being used to process accounting problems on an IBM 704. At about the same time Sutherland Management Consultants also began experimenting with decision tables. Their approach was to use the tables for problem specifications and then have the programmer code from the tables. In 1960 information about the experiences of General Electric with decision logic tables was presented at the Fall Joint Computer Conference. Several companies began experimenting with the use of tables shortly thereafter. A manual called DETAB-X was published in 1962 by the CODASYL Systems Development Committee. This manual described a decision table preprocessor that could accept the decision tables as input and give a form of COBOL coding as output. This was the first table processor to be generally available to computer users.

At a special seminar on decision tables held at the U.S. Bureau of the Census in September 1964, the seminar chairman, Morris J. Solomon (Chief, Operations Research Branch, Statistical Research Division, Bureau of the Census), told of some of the early work in the development of table processors:

"Our initial interest in decision tables was as a means of setting down and communicating specifications. As we studied the literature and talked to users, a number of very interesting possibilities emerged.

First, it was clear that decision tables lent themselves to mathematical treatment. Given the number of conditions, one could account for all the possible combinations and their corresponding actions on an analytical basis. One could devise mathematical algorithms which would point up redundancies and inconsistencies. Analogous routines had been used by designers of computers.

Second, there was the distinct possibility of having a computer capability of turning a decision table in prescribed form and language into a computer program. With such a table, subject matter persons might write a decision table which would be punched up and fed directly to a computer to be turned into usable coding. This in fact is the basis of the G.E. computer system which has been successfully used for several years. Our talks with G.E. users made this prospect both enticing and realistic.

Third, experiments with the decision table form, along mathematical lines, indicated that it is quite realistic to aim for processing of decision tables that would turn out very efficient if not optimum coding and we could expect progress to be cumulative. Mr. O'Brien and I worked out some logical systems that were promising. We communicated these to a RAND Corporation Mathematician, Mr. Sol Pollack. This work suggested some lines of attack which have resulted in some very promising algorithms for converting decision tables into efficient coding, taking into account the frequency of condition. There is every reason to believe that these approaches represent a highly promising development in computer programming. It is true that for the present the coding of decision tables by computer is tied to an English type language such as COBOL or FORTRAN and can be no better than the language used.

In any case, at present there are a large number of jobs where the volume of records is sufficiently small to warrant the use of English language programs, providing low cost programming and early completion can be realized. The definition of conditions where this is the case is an important area of future investigation."

## EVOLUTION AND REFINEMENT OF TABLE PROCESSORS

From DETAB-X came a newer, more sophisticated processor known as DETAB-65. This processor has been used successfully with IBM, Univac, and possibly other computers. The language of DETAB-65 is COBOL. It tests condition by condition.

General Electric has developed a processor, called TABSOL, that also tests condition by condition. The language is described as "almost COBOL"—near enough to use with COBOL programs.

The U.S. Bureau of the Census originally used a processor developed in cooperation with the Sperry Rand Corporation. CENTAB tested rule by rule and was used with COBOL programs. However, CENTAB has been replaced by a new processor, called TAB7C, that tests condition by condition and is used with FORTRAN programs. This processor has been called "a miracle of modification." The Research Analysis Corporation (RAC) of McLean, Virginia, developed a processor called TAB40. This processor tests condition by condition and is used with FORTRAN programs. Although it was written for use with IBM computers, Howard Fletcher, Systems Staff, U.S. Bureau of the Census, has (with the approval of RAC) successfully modified TAB40 into a new processor to be used with the Census Bureau's Univac computers. The resulting TAB7C is one of the most efficient table processors in use today. IBM has done much work in the area of decision logic tables and has developed a processor called FORTAB, which is used with FORTRAN programs.

Additional work is being done in the refinement of decision tables and their use. The U.S. American Standards Institute has an Ad Hoc Committee currently working on decision logic tables. Many government agencies as well as private business firms are conducting extensive experiments in the area.

The table processors mentioned above are by no means the only ones available. If one that exactly meets your requirements for equipment and programming language is not available, you can probably find one that can easily be modified to fit the situation, just as TAB40 was modified to TAB7C for use at the Census Bureau. It is important to remember that in determining which table processor is best for a given system the most important consideration is usually the programming language used.

## CONSIDERATIONS IN CHOOSING A PROCESSOR

In choosing a table processor several things must be considered. Probably the most important is the programming language that will be used. Most processors now available are used with FORTRAN and COBOL.

Hardware configurations using decision table processors range from an IBM 1401 with tapes to the largest computers available. Generally any computer capable of compiling a FORTRAN or COBOL program is also capable of using one of the available decision table processors.

Many factors affect the speed of machine processing of decision tables. These factors include the size of the tables themselves, the processor being used, and the speed of the computer. For example, the table processor for the IBM 1401 takes from 5 sec to 4 min to process each table. The average table is said to take approximately 1 min. Another processor that tested condition by condition on a Univac 1107 computer took 12 sec to translate decision tables consisting of a total of 145 lines to 345 lines of machine coding.

Some table processors using COBOL have a PERFORM feature, which allows a table to execute a remote table, much like a subroutine, and return to the original table. This is different from a GO TO (table name), which is a change of tables with no return to the original either implied or expected.

Some of the table processors using FORTRAN contain a DO

feature, which allows the execution of groupings of actions for given rules but does not send control to a different table.

In using a table processor that tests rule by rule one can save time by placing those rules most frequently encountered in the left-hand section of the table so that these will be tested first. Less frequently recurring rules should be to the right of the table. In testing condition by condition the ordering of the rules within the table has no real bearing. The table will test conditions as they appear, but often the order of the conditions is dictated by the number of responses to the condition needed to obtain a bifurcated arrangement.

The newer table processors have built-in automatic checks for possible redundancies and contradictions. They are "flagged" by the processor and a notation is made on the listing generated as output by the table-processing step. With older processors the tables must be examined by the designer, using methods suggested in other sections of this text, to spot omissions, redundancies, and contradictions.

## A LARGE JOB USING DECISION TABLES

### *Use of Decision Logic Tables in the 1964 Census of Agriculture*

The census itself was a staggering undertaking that involved 3,500,000 questionnaires, each containing a possibility of 355 questions. The survey was estimated to require a total of 53 man-years of programming and perhaps 3000 hr of computer time (Univac 1107). The enumeration was scheduled to take place in November 1964, with the first reports to be published by March 31, 1965.

In view of the fact that the questionnaire had so many elements, definable interrelationships among the various data elements were numerous. Because of this it was important to treat each record as an entity rather than to break it up into a series of smaller records. The great potential for errors and misinterpretations demanded that preparation of detailed narrative specifications for programming not even be seriously considered. It was decided that decision logic tables, though untried on a project of this size and nature, offered the most practical way of getting the job done in the allotted time. The finished job comprised about 600 pages of decision logic tables. These proved to be very effective for the purposes desired.

The general conclusion of the man who supervised the preparation of the computer programs for the 1964 Census of Agriculture was "The very extensive and comprehensive consistency checks and resulting adjustments in data considered desirable and profitable by the Agriculture Division could *NOT* have been computerized for the 1964 Census without the use of decision tables."

### A Time Comparison: Decision Tables versus Flow Charts

One data-processing staff conducted a study to compare the time involved in using conventional programming methods against the time involved in using decision logic tables. Two programmers, deemed to be equally experienced, were assigned similar programs. One of the comparisons follows:

|  | Conventional methods | Decision tables |
|---|---|---|
| Analysis | 80 hours | 40 hours |
| Research and learning | 40 | 21 |
| Documentation | 61 | 43 |
| Coding | 135 | 38 |
| Testing and debugging | 172 | 52 |
| Total | 488 | 194 |

In many cases the times for various steps down to coding will be about the same. But a considerable saving should always be apparent in coding, as well as in testing and debugging when decision logic tables are used.

# 4

# Conclusions

## PROSPECTS FOR DECISION LOGIC TABLES

It is apparent that decision logic tables are best suited to applications involving complex logic. This is true whether the application is manufacturing, scientific, data processing, or file processing. Any complex job can be undertaken with greater confidence by breaking the job into small segments, each of which can be studied, developed, and documented; then the segments can be reassembled as a whole.

With all the prospects that decision tables offer, "we should approach the day when new concepts required to get new jobs done or old jobs done in new ways can be almost automatically translated to computer coding. Then will computers become natural extension of the intellect, and change no longer a cause for despair." *

* R. Hornseth, "Decision Tables at the Bureau of the Census: History and Prospects," Seminar on Decision Tables, Washington, D.C., September, 1964, pp. 28–40.

**ADVANTAGES**

Decision logic tables provide a form and a precise procedure for naming conditions and actions for a given operation and showing their relationship. This permits easy examination, manipulation, and simplification of all aspects of the operation. By examining alternatives shown side by side, logic can be greatly improved. All aspects are considered and provisions must be made for each.

Decision tables serve as a checklist for procedural and specifications writers; the process of preparing the table forces them to plan better.

The tables not only are easy to prepare and update; they also lend themselves to independent review and change. Consequently changes in existing programs can be undertaken easily. Decision tables serve as documentation readily updated by any programmer; thus he is less dependent on the original programmer.

It is possible to program and debug more quickly and accurately from decision table documentation then from any other known type.

The ability of decision logic tables to serve as input to a computer and be converted into a coded program segment output makes their use especially attractive.


**DISADVANTAGES**

Like any new tool decision logic tables present some disadvantages. Despite the fact that they are easy to learn, prepare, and read, one must work extensively with them before he is truly efficient in their use. During such work, however, he will discover various "gimmicks" that make tables easier to construct and use.

In some situations when specifications have been presented to a programmer in decision table form, the programmer has complained of being downgraded to a clerk—a mere coder—since even logic was laid out by the specifications people in planning their work and the resulting tables. Such reluctance to change from the "traditional" methods of documentation often requires a good "public relations" job to implement the use of decision logic tables sucessfully in an established programming area.

Despite the fact that decision tables provide an effective means of describing logical structure and related actions, many problems are beyond their reach. The tables do not suggest significant broad relationships or assure that the actions specified are correct, logical, consistent, or even feasible. Even with the most elaborate internal checks and manipulation, decision tables can be no better than the wisdom and judgment that go into their preparation.

# Appendix A

---

## Exercises

The serious student should work the following exercises in order to gain a firm grasp of the decision table fundamentals. The material is purposely not arranged in order of difficulty. In fact, some of the exercises that at first glance appear to be very complicated are really simple.

Following the exercises there is a section containing sample solutions. But the solution shown for each example is not the only correct one, for each example could be solved in numerous ways. The form of the solutions has also been purposely varied to show the flexibility permitted in working with decision tables.

The solution of these exercises should make one aware of many techniques that can come only from experience.

### TOPCOAT?

A simple decision logic table is desired to illustrate the logic of the statement, "If foul weather is not forecast for today and the current temperature is not less than 50°, I will not wear my topcoat to work today."

## TOUR THE COMPUTER AREA?

In a certain government agency visitors are welcome to see the computers when they are in operation and are not processing classified material, and when a guide is available. Whenever visitors are not permitted to see the computer installation they are told the reason; for example, the guide is not available, the computers are not in operation, or classified material is being processed.

Show the above in a single decision logic table.

(for sample solution see page 67)

## HOSPITAL PLANNING

The input to this job is a file containing information about hospital facilities in all states east of the Mississippi River. A special report is desired for planning purposes in the tristate area of Georgia, Florida, and Alabama. In one column of the report will appear the names of all counties in Georgia having hospitals; immediately following the county name will be a number indicating the number of hospital beds in that county. When all counties have been listed in this manner, the total number of hospital beds in the state will be printed at the bottom of the listing. A similar column will be printed for Florida and a third for Alabama.

Write the decision logic table(s) necessary to generate this report.

(for sample solution see page 68)

## BARTENDER

Out of desperation the Smalls have had to hire an inexperienced bartender for their lawn party. Since the bartender doesn't know how to mix any drinks, the decision is made to offer only three choices: manhattan, martini, or screwdriver. Those who do not desire an alcoholic beverage should be offered a soft drink.

In order that the drinks will be mixed properly, prepare a decision table for the bartender to use when a drink is requested. Norms for drinks have been set as follows:

Manhattan: 3 parts bourbon, 1 part sweet vermouth
Martini: 3 parts gin, 1 part dry vermouth
Screwdriver: 1 part vodka, 2 parts orange juice.

(for sample solution see page 69)

## HIRING A STENOGRAPHER

The Acme Corporation needs a large number of stenographers who can take dictation at 90 words per min (or faster) and can also type a minimum of 50 words per min. The typing pool needs typists who can type a minimum of 50 words per min; shorthand is not required. Design a single decision table for hiring for these two positions. Hiring will be based strictly on typing and stenographic speeds.

## HIRING A RECEPTIONIST

The Globe Company needs a new receptionist. She must be able to type at least 50 words per min and take dictation at a minimum speed of 90 words per min. Although age or race is not important, it is desired that she be attractive. All applicants who meet typing requirements but are not considered attractive by the interviewer will be referred to the typing pool. No stenographers are currently required in any of the other offices.

Show the above in decision table form.

## HIRING A RECEPTIONIST ON A BUDGET

The Reform Corporation needs a receptionist for its new branch office. She will need to have typing skills of at least 50 words per min and dictation speed of 90 words per minute or greater. She should be attractive. Since the new branch is on a fairly tight budget she must be willing to start work at a salary not greater than $5500 a year.

Show the above in decision logic table form.

## STOCKHOLDERS

From a file of stockholder records, write the decision tables necessary to compile separate lists of stockholders owning more than 1000 shares of Waterburg Gas Works Stock. List A will contain names of individual stockholders; list B will contain names of banks holding stock; list C will show trust stockholders; and list D will show brokers holding stock.

## AUTOMATIC COAL MINING

An unmanned steam shovel in an automated coal mining operation can dig, scoop, and circle to dump what it has dug and scooped into a waiting truck.

Design a decision table to operate the shovel based on the following information. To ascertain how much loose coal has been dug, the shovel automatically measures after each dig motion. When it finds that a minimum of 2 ft of loose coal has been dug it scoops up a shovel full of coal, circles, and dumps it into a waiting truck. This scoop-circle-dump-return routine is automatically performed four times before the shovel resumes digging.

## TO SHIP OR NOT TO SHIP?

A firm that sells cleaning solvent to dry-cleaning establishments uses the following criteria for shipping credit orders. If the order is for one dozen barrels or less, if the credit department has approved the order, and if the quantity on hand is greater than or equal to the order size, ship the order. If the quantity on hand is not sufficient to fill such orders, show as "back order." If the order is for more than one dozen barrels, the order is to be automatically rejected. If order is for an acceptable number of barrels but the credit department has not approved it, reject the order.

## STUCK IN SNOW

Poor Mr. Thompson has his car stuck in the snow. He will attempt to rock it free. If he is successful in this, he will drive home. If not, he will see if a service station is in sight. If he sees one that appears to be open, he will walk to it and get the tow truck to free his car so that he can drive home; if the station is not open, or no station is in sight, he will have to resort to his chains. However, he's not sure if the chains are in the trunk of the car. If they are he'll put them on and drive home. If the chains are not in the trunk, he'll lock up his car and start walking toward home.

Show the possibilities involved in the above dilemma in decision logic table form.

## INVENTORY REPORT

An inventory report is generated by the computer in the following manner. Each transaction is punched into a single card; the computer uses the part number as the code for all processing. The card file contains an inventory-status card as well as all transaction cards for the preceding day. A card is read; then the computer makes a comparison between the card and the one just preceding it (which has been processed). If the part numbers are the same, the computer will tally any shipments shown on the card, tally any returns, and update current balance on hand. If the part numbers are not the same, it is obvious that all transactions for the preceding part number have been processed and the new card begins the processing for a new part number. At this point the program should direct that a line of the inventory report be printed to show the status of the part number just completed. An updated inventory-control card should also be punched to show the current status of the item; this card will be used as an input to the next running of the program.

## ELECTION PROBABILITY

In a city election for mayor, a team of election experts is attempting to predict the outcome. One of the experts studies the situation and comes up with the premise that no candidate who is either endorsed by labor or opposed by the daily newspaper can carry the Negro vote. No one can win the election without carrying the Negro bloc. Of the four candidates, Murphy and Johnson are endorsed by labor, and Johnson and McGee are not opposed by the press. Barnes is a long-time foe of the labor movement.

From these fragments of information, design a single decision table indicating who will probably win the election.

## MERGE (ASCENDING ORDER)

Two tapes (A and B) are each sorted into ascending order. Write a decision table to merge the two tapes (still in ascending order) into a single tape to be called MASTER.

## MERGE (DESCENDING ORDER)

Write decision table(s) to merge tape C with tape D in descending order to form a new tape called GOOD. Tape C and tape D have already been sorted into descending order.

## CURRENT STOCK INVENTORY

In keeping track of inventory stock the Stoner Company simplifies the problem in the following manner. If it is an actual physical removal of stock from the warehouse the quantity removed is subtracted from balance on hand. If goods are physically arriving at the warehouse (whether new stock or returned stock) the quantity is added to the balance on hand. Occasionally the taking of an inventory requires a stock adjustment to correct the balance on hand to reflect the true balance. If the stock adjustment is an "up adjustment" the quantity is added to the balance on hand; if a "down adjustment" the quantity is subtracted from the balance on hand.

Show the above in a single decision logic table.

## COMPARE

A program uses variables $A$, $B$, $C$, $F$, $M$, and $R$. Write a single decision logic table to accomplish the following.

Square $F$ and add the results to $M$ in cases when the value of $A$ is greater than the value of $B$. When the value of $A$ is not larger than the value of $B$, compare $A$ to $C$. If the value of $A$ is greater than that of $C$, cube $F$ and add the result to $M$. If the value of $A$ is smaller than both $B$ and $C$, add 1 to the counter $R$.

## THE AND LOGIC TABLE

In computers several logic tables are used. One of these is called the AND table. The table takes two true/false responses and combines them to give a single response using the following criteria:

True and True  = True
True and False  = False
False and False  = False
False and True  = False.

Show the logic in a decision table using two conditions: "True?" and "False?" Watch your step on this one!

## THE OR LOGIC TABLE

Another logic table used in computers is the OR table. This table takes true/false responses and combines them into a single response using the criteria shown below:

True or True  = True
True or False = True
False or False = True
False or True = True.

Show this logic in a decision logic table using the conditions "True?" and "False?" Again, watch your step.

## DRAFT ELIGIBLES

Illustrate the following situation in decision logic table form.

The Office of the Personnel wants to send questionnaires to all employees who *might* be affected by the draft. It needs a listing of all such employees who are between the ages of 19 and 26, even though they might have previously served. In addition to the master list of names, a tally of how many of those on the list are Caucasian, how many are Negro, how many are American Indian, and how many are "other" is needed. *All* personnel cards will be used as input to this job.

## FIND ACCEPTABLE RECORDS

In order to save future processing time, a special run is to be made to ascertain which records are acceptable and which are not. Those records in which field A equals field B or field C are acceptable. All others are rejects. Write a decision table to make the determination of acceptability; copy all acceptable records to a tape called GOOD and all unacceptable to a tape called REJEX.

## AUTO DEALER

An enterprising Volkswagen dealer in a small town carries a complete stock of engines but limited color selection in each body style. He carries three models: the Karmann Ghia, the "Bug," and the Fastback. When a customer orders a new car, if the color desired is available in the desired body style the dealer installs an engine and the customer can have one-day delivery. If the color is not in stock but is on order, the customer is promised one-week delivery. If the color is not in stock or on order, the car must be special-ordered, promised as one-month delivery.

Show the above in decision logic table(s).

## WHAT RANK?

Irma has just gotten a job in the Post Exchange at Fort Johnson. She knows how sensitive some military men are about their rank, and so she is determined to learn to identify their rank by the insignia they wear. Design a series of decision tables to aid Irma.

If a man wears his rank on his shoulder, he is an officer or warrant officer and she should address him as "Sir." She also should refer to him by rank, especially when writing his name on sales slips. If a man wears his rank on his sleeve in the form of stripes, he is an enlisted man. Men wearing two or more stripes are referred to in general as noncommissioned officers, but the number of stripes indicates actual rank. Those men wearing an eagle on the sleeve (or an eagle and stripe combination) hold specialist grades. These too are enlisted men, and each insignia denotes a different grade. The only grade not wearing grade insignia of any kind is a private, the lowest-paid enlisted man.

The lowest enlisted man who wears a stripe is the PFC (private first class), who wears a single stripe. Next is the corporal, with two. Three stripes indicate a sergeant; four indicate a staff sergeant. A sergeant first class wears five stripes. Six stripes denote a master sergeant. The highest-ranking enlisted man is the Sergeant major, who wears seven stripes enclosing a star.

It should be noted that such titles as Personnel Sergeant Major, Supply Sergeant, First Sergeant, and Sergeant of the Guard are not ranks; they are position titles.

Specialists have essentially the same rank structure as noncommissioned officers, who wear stripes. However, the insignia worn by a specialist is an eagle worn on the arm; the eagle may have small stripes with it to denote rank. The eagle alone denotes specialist four; with a single stripe, specialist five. A specialist six wears an eagle with two stripes; a specialist seven wear three stripes with his eagle. Specialist eights wear the eagle with four stripes, and the highest specialist grade, specialist nine, wears an eagle with five stripes.

An officer who wears a single gold bar is a second lieutenant; if he wears a single silver bar, he is a first lieutenant. Double silver bars denote a captain. A gold oak leaf is worn by a major; a silver oak leaf is worn by a lieutenant colonel. A colonel is sometimes referred to as a "bird colonel" because of the silver eagle he wears. Above the rank of colonel are five different types of generals: one gold star is worn by a brigadier general; two gold stars by a major general; three by a lieutenant general; four by a general; and five by a general of the armies. Irma might never encounter anyone wearing the top three grades because they are not that numerous.

Warrant officers wear special insignia in the same position as an officer. They may simply be referred to as "Warrant Officer Jones" or "Sir."

## INSURANCE PREMIUMS

Show all of the information reflected by the following table in decision logic table form.

| AGE | STATE OF HEALTH | | | |
|---|---|---|---|---|
| | EXCEL | GOOD | FAIR | POOR |
| Under 30 | 1.28 | 1.53 | 2.00 | 2.73 |
| 30–40 | 1.82 | 2.13 | 2.53 | 3.43 |
| 40–50 | 2.52 | 2.94 | 3.46 | 5.28 |
| 50–60 | 3.28 | 3.92 | 4.84 | 8.74 |
| 60+ | 5.23 | 6.44 | 7.60 | 10.94 |

## WHAT MADE THEM SICK?

During Spring holidays only six men remained in the fraternity house on Elm Street. On Tuesday the cook was surprised to learn that five of the six had been very ill the previous night. She asked each of the six to make a list of foods he had eaten the preceding day.

Jerry, a math major from the Bronx, listed cereal, tuna salad, turtle soup, canned pears, roast pork, cream pie, and coffee.

Fred, a serious drama student from Ohio, indicated that he had eaten roast pork, tuna salad, cream pie, tomato soup, milk, tossed salad, canned pears, and coffee.

Milk, canned pears, tuna salad, roast pork, turtle soup, mixed vegetables, cream pie, and tea were listed by Mike, a husky quarterback from Iowa.

Tom, a rabbinical student from Yonkers, listed milk and cereal, for breakfast; tomato soup, canned pears, and tea for lunch; and tuna salad, mixed vegetables, and tea for dinner.

Cereal, milk, and tea were breakfast foods for Art. During the remainder of the day he also ate tomato soup, tuna salad, roast pork, tossed salad, cream pie, and tea.

While in baseball training George was watching his diet. He had eaten cereal, coffee, milk, canned pears, roast pork, tossed salad, mixed vegetables, and turtle soup.

About 8:00 P.M. both Fred and Tom had begun to vomit. About an hour later Jerry became sick. Art was not sick at all. Mike and George each awakened in the wee hours of the next day with an upset stomach.

Since the cook is interested only in what actually was eaten and not in all possible combinations* of the 12 foods in question, plot a rule column for each student's diet. Then from the side-by-side comparisons determine which food *probably* was guilty.

## FLOWCHART TO DECISION LOGIC TABLE (NUMBER I)

Convert the following flowchart segment to decision logic table form.

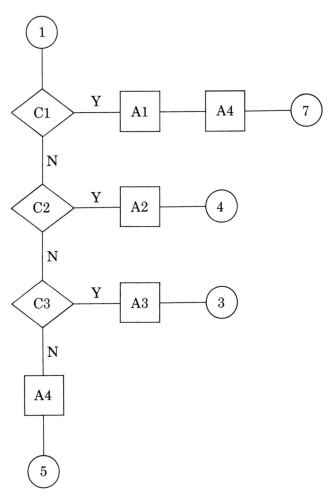

* The number of combinations possible is $2^{12}$ or 4096!

## FLOWCHART TO DECISION LOGIC TABLE (NUMBER II)

Draw a decision logic table which reflects the logic shown in the following segment.

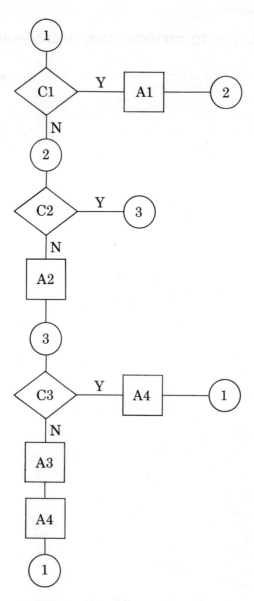

## SUGGESTED SOLUTIONS

### Topcoat?

| DECISION LOGIC TABLE | Job *DRESS*  Date<br>Prepared by *MAYBELL* | | | | | | | |
|---|---|---|---|---|---|---|---|---|
| *TOPCOAT* | *1* | *2* | *3* | *4* | | | | |
| *LESS THAN 50° OUTSIDE ?* | Y | Y | N | N | | | | |
| *FOUL  WEATHER  FORECAST ?* | Y | N | Y | N | | | | |
| *WEAR  TOPCOAT* | X | X | X | | | | | |
| *DO NOT  WEAR  TOPCOAT* | | | | X | | | | |
| | | | | | | | | |
| | | | | | | | | |
| | | | | | | | | |

### Tour the Computer Area?

| DECISION LOGIC TABLE | Job *PUBLIC RELATIONS*  Date<br>Prepared by *PAUL* | | | | | | | |
|---|---|---|---|---|---|---|---|---|
| *COMPUTER  TOUR* | *1* | *2* | *3* | *4* | | | | |
| *IS THE COMPUTER IN OPERATION ?* | Y | Y | Y | N | | | | |
| *IS CLASSIFIED  MATERIAL  BEING RUN ?* | Y | N | N | | | | | |
| *IS  A  GUIDE  AVAILABLE ?* | | Y | N | | | | | |
| *TOUR IS POSSIBLE* | | X | | | | | | |
| *NO TOUR ; COMPUTER NOT RUNNING* | | | | X | | | | |
| *NO TOUR ; PROCESSING  CLASSIFIED MATERIAL* | X | | | | | | | |
| *NO TOUR ; GUIDE NOT AVAILABLE* | | | X | | | | | |
| | | | | | | | | |
| | | | | | | | | |
| | | | | | | | | |

## Hospital Planning

| DECISION LOGIC TABLE | Job MEDICAL PLANNING    Date<br>Prepared by MORGAN | | | | | | | |
|---|---|---|---|---|---|---|---|---|
| HOSPITAL | | | | | | | | |
|  | 1 | 2 | 3 | 4 | 5 | | | |
| END OF FILE ? | Y | N | N | N | N | | | |
| COUNTY IN GEORGIA ? | | Y | N | N | N | | | |
| COUNTY IN FLORIDA ? | | | Y | N | N | | | |
| COUNTY IN ALABAMA ? | | | | Y | N | | | |
| LIST GA. COLUMN ; ADD TO GA. TOTAL | | X | | | | | | |
| LIST FLA. COLUMN ; ADD TO FLA. TOTAL | | | X | | | | | |
| LIST ALA. COLUMN ; ADD TO ALA. TOTAL | | | | X | | | | |
| NO INTEREST ; GO TO NEXT RECORD | | | | | X | | | |
| PRINT TOTAL FOR GEORGIA | X | | | | | | | |
| PRINT TOTAL FOR FLORIDA | X | | | | | | | |
| PRINT TOTAL FOR ALABAMA | X | | | | | | | |
| END OF JOB | X | | | | | | | |
|  | | | | | | | | |
|  | | | | | | | | |
|  | | | | | | | | |

## Bartender

| DECISION LOGIC TABLE | Job *PARTY*     Date<br>Prepared by   *SMALL* | | | | | | | |
|---|---|---|---|---|---|---|---|---|
| *DRINKS* | *1* | *2* | *3* | *4* | | | | |
| MANHATTAN ? | Y | N | N | N | | | | |
| MARTINI ? | | Y | N | N | | | | |
| SCREWDRIVER ? | | | Y | N | | | | |
| MIX 3 PARTS BOURBON, 1 SWEET VERMOUTH | X | | | | | | | |
| MIX 3 PARTS GIN, 1 DRY VERMOUTH | | X | | | | | | |
| MIX 1 PART VODKA, 2 ORANGE JUICE | | | X | | | | | |
| OFFER GUEST A SOFT DRINK | | | | X | | | | |
| | | | | | | | | |
| | | | | | | | | |

## Hiring a Stenographer

| DECISION LOGIC TABLE | Job *PLACEMENT* Date<br>Prepared by *GREEN* | | | | | | | |
|---|---|---|---|---|---|---|---|---|
| *STENO / TYPIST* | *1* | *2* | *3* | | | | | |
| TYPE ≥ 50 WPM ? | Y | Y | N | | | | | |
| SHORTHAND ≥ 90 WPM ? | Y | N | | | | | | |
| HIRE AS STENO | X | | | | | | | |
| HIRE AS TYPIST | | X | | | | | | |
| DO NOT HIRE | | | X | | | | | |
| | | | | | | | | |
| | | | | | | | | |

## Hiring a Receptionist

| DECISION LOGIC TABLE | Job *PLACEMENT* Date<br>Prepared by  *GREEN* | | | | | | | |
|---|---|---|---|---|---|---|---|---|
| *RECEPTIONIST* | 1 | 2 | 3 | 4 | 5 | | | |
| ATTRACTIVE ? | Y | Y | Y | N | N | | | |
| TYPE ≥ 50 WPM ? | Y | Y | N | Y | N | | | |
| SHORTHAND ≥ 90 WPM ? | Y | N | | | | | | |
| HIRE | X | | | | | | | |
| DO NOT HIRE | | X | X | X | X | | | |
| REFER TO TYPING POOL | | X | | X | | | | |
| | | | | | | | | |
| | | | | | | | | |

## Hiring a Receptionist on a Budget

| DECISION LOGIC TABLE | Job *PLACEMENT* Date<br>Prepared by  *MARGE* | | | | | | | |
|---|---|---|---|---|---|---|---|---|
| *BRANCH RECEPTIONIST* | 1 | 2 | 3 | 4 | 5 | | | |
| ATTRACTIVE ? | N | Y | Y | Y | Y | | | |
| TYPE ≥ 50 WPM ? | | N | Y | Y | Y | | | |
| SHORTHAND ≥ 90 WPM ? | | | N | Y | Y | | | |
| SALARY REQUIREMENTS ≤ $5500 ? | | | | N | Y | | | |
| HIRE | | | | | X | | | |
| DO NOT HIRE | X | X | X | X | | | | |
| | | | | | | | | |
| | | | | | | | | |

## Stockholders

| DECISION LOGIC TABLE | | Job *WATERBURY*  Date *12-31-66*<br>Prepared by  *KAPLAN* | | | | | | | | | |
|---|---|---|---|---|---|---|---|---|---|---|---|
| *STOCKS* | | | | | | | | | | | |
| | | 1 | 2 | 3 | 4 | 5 | | | | | |
| *NUMBER OF SHARES > 1000 ?* | | N | Y | Y | Y | Y | | | | | |
| *HELD BY AN INDIVIDUAL ?* | | | Y | N | N | N | | | | | |
| *HELD BY A BANK ?* | | | | Y | N | N | | | | | |
| *HELD BY A TRUST COMPANY ?* | | | | | Y | N | | | | | |
| *READ NEXT RECORD* | | X | | | | | | | | | |
| *WRITE NAME ON LIST A* | | | X | | | | | | | | |
| *WRITE NAME ON LIST B* | | | | X | | | | | | | |
| *WRITE NAME ON LIST C* | | | | | X | | | | | | |
| *WRITE NAME ON LIST D* | | | | | | X | | | | | |
| | | | | | | | | | | | |
| | | | | | | | | | | | |

## Automatic Coal Mining

| DECISION LOGIC TABLE | | Job *MINING*      Date<br>Prepared by  *GEORGE* | | | |
|---|---|---|---|---|---|
| *DIG* | | | | | |
| | | 1 | 2 | | |
| *TWO FEET OF LOOSE COAL ?* | | Y | N | | |
| *SCOOP, CIRCLE, DUMP ROUTINE* | | X | | | |
| *DIG* | | | X | | |
| | | | | | |
| | | | | | |

## To Ship or Not to Ship

| DECISION LOGIC TABLE | Job SALES  Date 4-22-67  Prepared by BARRY | | | | | | | | | |
|---|---|---|---|---|---|---|---|---|---|---|
| CREDIT ORDERS | 1 | 2 | 3 | 4 | | | | | | |
| IS ORDER ≤ ORDER LIMIT ? | N | Y | Y | Y | | | | | | |
| CREDIT APPROVED ? | | N | Y | Y | | | | | | |
| QUANTITY ON HAND ≥ ORDER SIZE ? | | | N | Y | | | | | | |
| REJECT ORDER | X | X | | | | | | | | |
| SHIP ORDER | | | | X | | | | | | |
| BACK ORDER | | | X | | | | | | | |
| | | | | | | | | | | |
| | | | | | | | | | | |

## Stuck in Snow

| DECISION LOGIC TABLE | Job STUCK  Date 12-12-66  Prepared by THOMPSON | | | | | | | | | |
|---|---|---|---|---|---|---|---|---|---|---|
| TRY | 1 | 2 | | | | | | | | |
| ABLE TO ROCK FREE ? | Y | N | | | | | | | | |
| DRIVE HOME | X | | | | | | | | | |
| GO TO HOPE TABLE | | X | | | | | | | | |
| | | | | | | | | | | |
| | | | | | | | | | | |

## Stuck in Snow (*Continued*)

| DECISION LOGIC TABLE | | Job *STUCK*     Date *12-12-66* | | | | | | | | | |
|---|---|---|---|---|---|---|---|---|---|---|---|
| | | Prepared by   *THOMPSON* | | | | | | | | | |
| *HOPE* | | 1 | 2 | 3 | | | | | | | |
| GAS STATION IN SIGHT ? | | Y | Y | N | | | | | | | |
| DOES IT APPEAR TO BE OPEN ? | | Y | N | | | | | | | | |
| WALK OVER TO GET TOW TRUCK | | X | | | | | | | | | |
| GO TO CHAINS TABLE | | | X | X | | | | | | | |
| | | | | | | | | | | | |
| | | | | | | | | | | | |
| | | | | | | | | | | | |

## Stuck in Snow (*Continued*)

| DECISION LOGIC TABLE | | Job *STUCK*     Date *12-12-66* | | | | | | | | | |
|---|---|---|---|---|---|---|---|---|---|---|---|
| | | Prepared by   *THOMPSON* | | | | | | | | | |
| *CHAINS* | | 1 | 2 | | | | | | | | |
| CHAINS IN TRUNK ? | | Y | N | | | | | | | | |
| PUT THEM ON CAR, DRIVE HOME | | X | | | | | | | | | |
| LOCK CAR, WALK TOWARD HOME | | | X | | | | | | | | |
| | | | | | | | | | | | |
| | | | | | | | | | | | |
| | | | | | | | | | | | |

## Inventory Report

| DECISION LOGIC TABLE | Job *WAREHOUSE*  Date *6-5-65*<br>Prepared by *MARK* | | | | | | | | | |
|---|---|---|---|---|---|---|---|---|---|---|
| *INVENTORY REPORT GENERATOR* | *1* | *2* | | | | | | | | |
| *NEW PART NUMBER ?* | Y | N | | | | | | | | |
| *PRINT LINE FOR PRIOR STOCK NUMBER* | X | | | | | | | | | |
| *PUNCH UPDATED CARD FOR PRIOR NUMBER* | X | | | | | | | | | |
| *COMPUTE SHIPMENTS THIS STOCK NUMBER* | | X | | | | | | | | |
| *COMPUTE RETURNS THIS STOCK NUMBER* | | X | | | | | | | | |
| *COMPUTE CURRENT BALANCE THIS NUMBER* | | X | | | | | | | | |
| | | | | | | | | | | |
| | | | | | | | | | | |
| | | | | | | | | | | |

## Election Probability

| DECISION LOGIC TABLE | Job *ELECTION*  Date<br>Prepared by *DEWEY* | | | | | | | |
|---|---|---|---|---|---|---|---|---|
| *MAYOR* | *MURPHY*<br>*1* | *JOHNSON*<br>*2* | *BARNES*<br>*3* | *McGEE*<br>*4* | | | | |
| *ENDORSED BY LABOR ?* | Y | Y | N | N | | | | |
| *OPPOSED BY PRESS ?* | Y | N | Y | N | | | | |
| *CANNOT CARRY NEGRO VOTE (SHOULD NOT WIN)* | X | X | X | | | | | |
| *SHOULD CARRY NEGRO VOTE (SHOULD WIN)* | | | | X | | | | |
| | | | | | | | | |
| | | | | | | | | |

## Merge (Ascending Order)

| DECISION LOGIC TABLE | Job *MERGE*     Date | | | |
|---|---|---|---|---|
| | Prepared by *GOODSON* | | | |
| *ASCENDING* | | | | |
| | *1* | *2* | | |
| *"A" LESS THAN OR EQUAL TO "B" ?* | Y | N | | |
| *COPY "A" TO "MASTER"; ADVANCE "A" TO NEXT REC.* | X | | | |
| *COPY "B" TO "MASTER"; ADVANCE "B" TO NEXT REC.* | | X | | |
| | | | | |
| | | | | |

## Merge (Descending Order)

| DECISION LOGIC TABLE | Job *MERGE*     Date | | | |
|---|---|---|---|---|
| | Prepared by *GOODSON* | | | |
| *DESCENDING* | | | | |
| | *1* | *2* | | |
| *"C" GREATER THAN "D" ?* | Y | N | | |
| *COPY "C" TO "GOOD"; ADVANCE "C" TO NEXT REC.* | X | | | |
| *COPY "D" TO "GOOD"; ADVANCE "D" TO NEXT REC.* | | X | | |
| | | | | |
| | | | | |

## Current Stock Inventory

| DECISION LOGIC TABLE | Job *WAREHOUSE* Date<br>Prepared by *FRED* | | | | | | | |
|---|---|---|---|---|---|---|---|---|
| *INVENTORY* | *1* | *2* | *3* | *4* | | | | |
| *WITHDRAWAL FROM STOCK ?* | Y | N | N | N | | | | |
| *RECEIPT OF STOCK ?* | | Y | N | N | | | | |
| *AN "UP" ADJUSTMENT ?* | | | Y | N | | | | |
| *SUBTRACT QUANTITY FROM BALANCE* | X | | | X | | | | |
| *ADD QUANTITY TO BALANCE* | | X | X | | | | | |
| | | | | | | | | |
| | | | | | | | | |
| | | | | | | | | |

## Compare

| DECISION LOGIC TABLE | Job *CODER* Date<br>Prepared by *MIKE* | | | | | | | |
|---|---|---|---|---|---|---|---|---|
| *COMPARE* | *1* | *2* | *3* | | | | | |
| *"A" GREATER THAN "B" ?* | Y | N | N | | | | | |
| *"A" GREATER THAN "C" ?* | | Y | N | | | | | |
| *SQUARE "F"; ADD RESULT TO "M"* | X | | | | | | | |
| *CUBE "F"; ADD RESULT TO "M"* | | X | | | | | | |
| *ADD 1 TO "R"* | | | X | | | | | |
| | | | | | | | | |
| | | | | | | | | |
| | | | | | | | | |

## The AND Logic Table

| DECISION LOGIC TABLE | | Job *LOGIC*   Date | | | | | | | |
|---|---|---|---|---|---|---|---|---|---|
| | | Prepared by *REM* | | | | | | | |
| *AND* | | 1 | 2 | 3 | 4 | | | | |
| TRUE ? | | Y | Y | N | N | | | | |
| FALSE ? | | Y | N | Y | N | | | | |
| RESULT IS TRUE | | | X | | | | | | |
| RESULT IS FALSE | | X | | X | X | | | | |
| | | | | | | | | | |
| | | | | | | | | | |

## The OR Logic Table

| DECISION LOGIC TABLE | | Job *LOGIC*   Date | | | | | | | |
|---|---|---|---|---|---|---|---|---|---|
| | | Prepared by *REM* | | | | | | | |
| *OR* | | 1 | 2 | 3 | 4 | | | | |
| TRUE ? | | Y | Y | N | N | | | | |
| FALSE ? | | Y | N | Y | N | | | | |
| RESULT IS TRUE | | X | X | | X | | | | |
| RESULT IS FALSE | | | | X | | | | | |
| | | | | | | | | | |
| | | | | | | | | | |

## Draft Eligibles

| DECISION LOGIC TABLE | Job *SERVICE*   Date<br>Prepared by *HERSHEY* | | | | | | | |
|---|---|---|---|---|---|---|---|---|
| *DRAFT* | | | | | | | | |
| | *1* | *2* | *3* | *4* | *5* | *6* | | |
| MALE ? | Y | Y | Y | Y | Y | N | | |
| AGE ≥ 19 AND ≤ 26 ? | Y | Y | Y | Y | N | | | |
| CAUCASIAN ? | Y | N | N | N | | | | |
| NEGRO ? | | Y | N | N | | | | |
| AMERICAN INDIAN ? | | | Y | N | | | | |
| WRITE NAME ON LIST | X | X | X | X | | | | |
| TALLY A CAUCASIAN | X | | | | | | | |
| TALLY A NEGRO | | X | | | | | | |
| TALLY AN AMERICAN INDIAN | | | X | | | | | |
| TALLY AN "OTHER" | | | | X | | | | |
| REJECT | | | | | X | X | | |
| | | | | | | | | |
| | | | | | | | | |

## Find Acceptable Records

| DECISION LOGIC TABLE | Job *PROCESS*   Date<br>Prepared by *RANDY* | | | | | | | |
|---|---|---|---|---|---|---|---|---|
| *DETERMINE* | | | | | | | | |
| | *1* | *2* | *3* | | | | | |
| "A" EQUAL "B" ? | Y | N | N | | | | | |
| "A" EQUAL "C" ? | | Y | N | | | | | |
| COPY RECORD TO "GOOD" | X | X | | | | | | |
| COPY RECORD TO "REJEX" | | | X | | | | | |
| | | | | | | | | |
| | | | | | | | | |

## Auto Dealer

| DECISION LOGIC TABLE | Job *VOLKS* Date<br>Prepared by *KNAUS* | | | | | | | |
|---|---|---|---|---|---|---|---|---|
| *TYPE* | *1* | *2* | | | | | | |
| *SPORTS CAR ?* | Y | N | | | | | | |
| *GO TO KGHIA TABLE* | X | | | | | | | |
| *GO TO BUG TABLE* | | X | | | | | | |
| | | | | | | | | |
| | | | | | | | | |
| | | | | | | | | |

## Auto Dealer (Continued)

| DECISION LOGIC TABLE | Job *VOLKS* Date<br>Prepared by *KNAUS* | | | | | | | |
|---|---|---|---|---|---|---|---|---|
| *KGHIA* | *1* | *2* | *3* | | | | | |
| *COLOR AVAILABLE ?* | Y | N | N | | | | | |
| *DUE IN WITHIN 1 WEEK ?* | | Y | N | | | | | |
| *DELIVER WHEN DESIRED* | X | | | | | | | |
| *PROMISE DELIVERY "NEXT WEEK"* | | X | | | | | | |
| *WRITE A SPECIAL ORDER* | | | X | | | | | |
| | | | | | | | | |
| | | | | | | | | |
| | | | | | | | | |

## Auto Dealer *(Continued)*

| DECISION LOGIC TABLE | Job *VOLKS*    Date<br>Prepared by *KNAUS* | | | | | | | |
|---|---|---|---|---|---|---|---|---|
| *BUG* | | | | | | | | |
| | 1 | 2 | 3 | 4 | 5 | 6 | | |
| *BUG ?* | Y | Y | Y | N | N | N | | |
| *COLOR AVAILABLE ?* | Y | N | N | N | N | Y | | |
| *DUE IN WITHIN 1 WEEK ?* | | Y | N | N | Y | | | |
| *DELIVER WHEN DESIRED* | X | | | | | X | | |
| *PROMISE DELIVERY IN 1 WEEK* | | X | | | X | | | |
| *SPECIAL ORDER BUG* | | | X | | | | | |
| *SPECIAL ORDER SEDAN* | | | | X | | | | |
| | | | | | | | | |
| | | | | | | | | |

## What Rank?

| DECISION LOGIC TABLE | Job *RANK*    Date *6-4-66*<br>Prepared by *PETER* | | | | | | | | | |
|---|---|---|---|---|---|---|---|---|---|---|
| *INSIGNIA* | | | | | | | | | | |
| | 1 | 2 | 3 | 4 | | | | | | |
| *WORN ON SHOULDER ?* | Y | N | N | N | | | | | | |
| *WORN ON SLEEVE ?* | | N | Y | Y | | | | | | |
| *STRIPES ?* | | | Y | N | | | | | | |
| *GO TO OFFICER TABLE* | X | | | | | | | | | |
| *RANK IS PRIVATE* | | X | | | | | | | | |
| *GO TO STRIPES TABLE* | | | X | | | | | | | |
| *GO TO EAGLE TABLE* | | | | X | | | | | | |
| | | | | | | | | | | |
| | | | | | | | | | | |

## What Rank? *(Continued)*

| DECISION LOGIC TABLE | Job *RANK*  Date *6-4-66* Prepared by *PETER* | | | | | | | | | |
|---|---|---|---|---|---|---|---|---|---|---|
| STRIPES | 1 | 2 | 3 | 4 | 5 | 6 | 7 | 8 | | |
| SINGLE STRIPE ? | Y | N | N | N | N | N | N | N | | |
| TWO STRIPES ? | | Y | N | N | N | N | N | N | | |
| THREE STRIPES ? | | | Y | N | N | N | N | N | | |
| FOUR STRIPES ? | | | | Y | N | N | N | N | | |
| FIVE STRIPES ? | | | | | Y | N | N | N | | |
| SIX STRIPES ? | | | | | | Y | N | N | | |
| SEVEN STRIPES ? | | | | | | | Y | N | | |
| PRIVATE FIRST CLASS | X | | | | | | | | | |
| CORPORAL | | X | | | | | | | | |
| SERGEANT | | | X | | | | | | | |
| STAFF-SERGEANT | | | | X | | | | | | |
| SERGEANT FIRST CLASS | | | | | X | | | | | |
| MASTER SERGEANT | | | | | | X | | | | |
| SERGEANT-MAJOR | | | | | | | X | | | |
| GOOF ! | | | | | | | | X | | |
| | | | | | | | | | | |
| | | | | | | | | | | |

## What Rank? *(Continued)*

| DECISION LOGIC TABLE | Job *RANK*  Date *6-4-66* <br> Prepared by *PETER* | | | | | | | | | |
|---|---|---|---|---|---|---|---|---|---|---|
| *EAGLE* | 1 | 2 | 3 | 4 | 5 | 6 | 7 | | | |
| *EAGLE ALONE ?* | Y | N | N | N | N | N | N | | | |
| *EAGLE WITH ONE STRIPE ?* | | Y | N | N | N | N | N | | | |
| *EAGLE WITH TWO STRIPES ?* | | | Y | N | N | N | N | | | |
| *EAGLE WITH THREE STRIPES ?* | | | | Y | N | N | N | | | |
| *EAGLE WITH FOUR STRIPES ?* | | | | | Y | N | N | | | |
| *EAGLE WITH FIVE STRIPES ?* | | | | | | Y | N | | | |
| *SPECIALIST FOUR* | X | | | | | | | | | |
| *SPECIALIST FIVE* | | X | | | | | | | | |
| *SPECIALIST SIX* | | | X | | | | | | | |
| *SPECIALIST SEVEN* | | | | X | | | | | | |
| *SPECIALIST EIGHT* | | | | | X | | | | | |
| *SPECIALIST NINE* | | | | | | X | | | | |
| *GOOF !* | | | | | | | X | | | |
| | | | | | | | | | | |
| | | | | | | | | | | |
| | | | | | | | | | | |

## What Rank? (Continued)

| DECISION LOGIC TABLE | Job RANK    Date 6-4-66 | | | | | | | | | | | |
|---|---|---|---|---|---|---|---|---|---|---|---|---|
| | Prepared by PETER | | | | | | | | | | | |
| **OFFICER** | | | | | | | | | | | | |
| | 1 | 2 | 3 | 4 | 5 | 6 | 7 | 8 | 9 | 10 | 11 | 12 |
| 1 GOLD BAR ? | Y | N | N | N | N | N | N | N | N | N | N | N |
| 1 SILVER BAR ? | | Y | N | N | N | N | N | N | N | N | N | N |
| 2 SILVER BARS ? | | | Y | N | N | N | N | N | N | N | N | N |
| GOLD OAK LEAF ? | | | | Y | N | N | N | N | N | N | N | N |
| SILVER OAK LEAF ? | | | | | Y | N | N | N | N | N | N | N |
| SILVER EAGLE ? | | | | | | Y | N | N | N | N | N | N |
| 1 GOLD STAR ? | | | | | | | Y | N | N | N | N | N |
| 2 GOLD STARS ? | | | | | | | | Y | N | N | N | N |
| 3 GOLD STARS ? | | | | | | | | | Y | N | N | N |
| 4 GOLD STARS ? | | | | | | | | | | Y | N | N |
| 5 GOLD STARS ? | | | | | | | | | | | Y | N |
| SECOND LIEUTENANT | X | | | | | | | | | | | |
| FIRST LIEUTENANT | | X | | | | | | | | | | |
| CAPTAIN | | | X | | | | | | | | | |
| MAJOR | | | | X | | | | | | | | |
| LIEUTENANT-COLONEL | | | | | X | | | | | | | |
| COLONEL | | | | | | X | | | | | | |
| BRIGADIER-GENERAL | | | | | | | X | | | | | |
| MAJOR-GENERAL | | | | | | | | X | | | | |
| LIEUTENANT-GENERAL | | | | | | | | | X | | | |
| GENERAL | | | | | | | | | | X | | |
| GENERAL-OF-THE-ARMIES | | | | | | | | | | | X | |
| WARRANT OFFICER | | | | | | | | | | | | X |

## Insurance Premiums

| DECISION LOGIC TABLE | Job *INSURANCE*  Date *9-2-66* <br> Prepared by *BILL RICHMOND* | | | | | | | | | | |
|---|---|---|---|---|---|---|---|---|---|---|---|
| STATE OF HEALTH | | | | | | | | | | | |
| | 1 | 2 | 3 | 4 | | | | | | | |
| IS HEALTH EXCELLENT ? | Y | N | N | N | | | | | | | |
| IS HEALTH GOOD ? | | Y | N | N | | | | | | | |
| IS HEALTH FAIR ? | | | Y | N | | | | | | | |
| GO TO ERATE TABLE | X | | | | | | | | | | |
| GO TO GRATE TABLE | | X | | | | | | | | | |
| GO TO FRATE TABLE | | | X | | | | | | | | |
| GO TO PRATE TABLE | | | | X | | | | | | | |
| | | | | | | | | | | | |
| | | | | | | | | | | | |
| | | | | | | | | | | | |

## Insurance Premiums (Continued)

| DECISION LOGIC TABLE | Job *INSURANCE*  Date *9-2-66* <br> Prepared by *BILL RICHMOND* | | | | | | | | | | |
|---|---|---|---|---|---|---|---|---|---|---|---|
| ERATE TABLE | | | | | | | | | | | |
| | 1 | 2 | 3 | 4 | 5 | | | | | | |
| AGE LESS THAN 30 ? | Y | N | N | N | N | | | | | | |
| AGE .GE. 30 AND .LT. 40 ? | | Y | N | N | N | | | | | | |
| AGE .GE. 40 AND .LT. 50 ? | | | Y | N | N | | | | | | |
| AGE .GE. 50 AND .LT. 60 ? | | | | Y | N | | | | | | |
| RATE = $1.28 | X | | | | | | | | | | |
| RATE = $1.82 | | X | | | | | | | | | |
| RATE = $2.52 | | | X | | | | | | | | |
| RATE = $3.28 | | | | X | | | | | | | |
| RATE = $5.23 | | | | | X | | | | | | |
| | | | | | | | | | | | |
| | | | | | | | | | | | |
| | | | | | | | | | | | |

## Insurance Premiums (Continued)

| DECISION LOGIC TABLE | Job *INSURANCE*  Date *9-2-66* |
| --- | --- |
| | Prepared by *BILL RICHMOND* |

**GRATE TABLE**

| | 1 | 2 | 3 | 4 | 5 | | | | |
| --- | --- | --- | --- | --- | --- | --- | --- | --- | --- |
| AGE LESS THAN 30 ? | Y | N | N | N | N | | | | |
| AGE .GE. 30 AND .LT. 40 ? | | Y | N | N | N | | | | |
| AGE .GE. 40 AND .LT. 50 ? | | | Y | N | N | | | | |
| AGE .GE. 50 AND .LT. 60 ? | | | | Y | N | | | | |
| RATE = $ 1.53 | X | | | | | | | | |
| RATE = $ 2.13 | | X | | | | | | | |
| RATE = $ 2.94 | | | X | | | | | | |
| RATE = $ 3.92 | | | | X | | | | | |
| RATE = $ 6.44 | | | | | X | | | | |
| | | | | | | | | | |
| | | | | | | | | | |
| | | | | | | | | | |

## Insurance Premiums (Continued)

| DECISION LOGIC TABLE | Job *INSURANCE*  Date *9-2-66* |
| --- | --- |
| | Prepared by *BILL RICHMOND* |

**FRATE TABLE**

| | 1 | 2 | 3 | 4 | 5 | | | | |
| --- | --- | --- | --- | --- | --- | --- | --- | --- | --- |
| AGE LESS THAN 30 ? | Y | N | N | N | N | | | | |
| AGE .GE. 30 AND .LT. 40 ? | | Y | N | N | N | | | | |
| AGE .GE. 40 AND .LT. 50 ? | | | Y | N | N | | | | |
| AGE .GE. 50 AND .LT. 60 ? | | | | Y | N | | | | |
| RATE = $ 2.00 | X | | | | | | | | |
| RATE = $ 2.53 | | X | | | | | | | |
| RATE = $ 3.46 | | | X | | | | | | |
| RATE = $ 4.84 | | | | X | | | | | |
| RATE = $ 7.60 | | | | | X | | | | |
| | | | | | | | | | |
| | | | | | | | | | |
| | | | | | | | | | |

## *Insurance Premiums (Continued)*

| DECISION LOGIC TABLE | Job *INSURANCE* Date *9-2-66* <br> Prepared by *BILL RICHMOND* | | | | | | | | | |
|---|---|---|---|---|---|---|---|---|---|---|
| *PRATE TABLE* | | | | | | | | | | |
| | *1* | *2* | *3* | *4* | *5* | | | | | |
| *AGE LESS THAN 30 ?* | Y | N | N | N | N | | | | | |
| *AGE .GE. 30 AND .LT. 40 ?* | | Y | N | N | N | | | | | |
| *AGE .GE. 40 AND .LT. 50 ?* | | | Y | N | N | | | | | |
| *AGE .GE. 50 AND .LT. 60 ?* | | | | Y | N | | | | | |
| *RATE = $ 2.73* | X | | | | | | | | | |
| *RATE = $ 3.43* | | X | | | | | | | | |
| *RATE = $ 5.28* | | | X | | | | | | | |
| *RATE = $ 8.74* | | | | X | | | | | | |
| *RATE = $ 10.94* | | | | | X | | | | | |
| | | | | | | | | | | |
| | | | | | | | | | | |

## What Made Them Sick?

| DECISION LOGIC TABLE | Job *SPECIAL*    Date | | | | | | | | | |
|---|---|---|---|---|---|---|---|---|---|---|
| | Prepared by *MAC* | | | | | | | | | |
| SICK | JERRY | FRED | MIKE | TOM | ART | GEORGE | | | | |
| CEREAL ? | Y | | | Y | Y | Y | | | | |
| TUNA SALAD ? | Y | Y | Y | Y | Y | | | | | |
| TURTLE SOUP ? | Y | | Y | | | Y | | | | |
| TOMATO SOUP ? | | Y | | Y | Y | | | | | |
| MIXED VEGETABLES ? | | | Y | | | Y | | | | |
| ROAST PORK ? | Y | Y | Y | | Y | Y | | | | |
| CANNED PEARS ? | Y | Y | Y | Y | | Y | | | | |
| TOSSED SALAD ? | | Y | | | Y | Y | | | | |
| CREAM PIE ? | Y | Y | Y | Y | Y | | | | | |
| COFFEE ? | Y | Y | | | | Y | | | | |
| TEA ? | | | Y | Y | Y | | | | | |
| MILK ? | | Y | Y | Y | | Y | | | | |
| SICK | X | X | X | X | | X | | | | |
| NOT SICK | | | | | X | | | | | |
| | | | | | | | | | | |
| | | | | | | | | | | |
| | | | | | | | | | | |

## Flowchart to Decision Logic Table (Number I)

| DECISION LOGIC TABLE | Job CONVERT    Date 5-1-67<br>Prepared by Mc GREGOR | | | | | | | | |
|---|---|---|---|---|---|---|---|---|---|
| FLOWSEG I | 1 | 2 | 3 | 4 | | | | | |
| CONDITION 1 ? | Y | N | N | N | | | | | |
| CONDITION 2 ? | | Y | N | N | | | | | |
| CONDITION 3 ? | | | Y | N | | | | | |
| ACTION 1 | X | | | | | | | | |
| ACTION 2 | | X | | | | | | | |
| ACTION 3 | | | X | | | | | | |
| ACTION 4 | X | | | X | | | | | |
| | | | | | | | | | |
| | | | | | | | | | |

## Flowchart to Decision Logic Table (Number II)

| DECISION LOGIC TABLE | Job CONVERT    Date 5-1-67<br>Prepared by Mc GREGOR | | | | | | | | |
|---|---|---|---|---|---|---|---|---|---|
| SEG II | 1 | 2 | 3 | 4 | 5 | 6 | 7 | 8 | |
| CONDITION 1 ? | Y | Y | Y | Y | N | N | N | N | |
| CONDITION 2 ? | Y | Y | N | N | Y | Y | N | N | |
| CONDITION 3 ? | Y | N | Y | N | Y | N | Y | N | |
| ACTION 1 | X | X | X | X | | | | | |
| ACTION 2 | – | | | X | | | X | X | |
| ACTION 3 | | X | | X | | X | | X | |
| ACTION 4 | X | X | X | X | X | X | X | X | |
| | | | | | | | | | |
| | | | | | | | | | |

# Appendix B

# Glossary

**Action**   Something to be done predicated on the responses to the conditions in the table. Action may be computations, movement of data, and so on.

**Action entry**   The lower right quadrant of the table. The only entry permitted in this section for tables in limited entry format is an "X." The "X," placed opposite an action, indicates that the action is to be taken; if there is no entry opposite the action, the action is not to be taken.

**Action stub**   The lower left quadrant of the body of the table. Listed here in narrative form are the actions to be taken, which depend on the conditions in the condition stub above. Entries may be computations, tallying, data movement, and so on.

**Bifurcation**   An arrangement whereby each condition tested has "yes" answers grouped together and "no" answers grouped together to form paths. Each condition tested will lead to testing of a subsequent condition or to an action or actions to be taken. This arrangement is required in order to be able to test a table condition by condition.

**Body of the table**   That part which contains all information relative to conditions and actions. Specifically, the body includes the condition stub, the condition entry, the action stub, and the action entry portions of the table.

**CENTAB**   A discussion table processor developed jointly by the U.S. Bureau of the Census and the Sperry Rand Corporation. Tests are made rule by rule; results are COBOL.

**COBOL**   Programming language. Name derived from COmmon Business-Oriented Language.

**Condition**   A test or a decision to be made as part of the logic or processing of a problem. It should be stated in question form and answered "yes" or "no" when working in limited-entry tables.

**Condition-by-condition testing**   A method of testing data against a decision table, which involves the checking of each condition in a sequential manner until all relevant conditions have been tested. The appropriate action or actions are then apparent. The number of tests will never exceed the number of conditions in the table.

**Condition entry**   The upper right quadrant of the body of the decision table. This section contains responses to questions asked in the condition stub. In limited-entry tables entries in this area are restricted to "Y" (yes), "N" (no), and blank (not examined).

**Condition stub**   The upper left quadrant of the body of the decision table. All the conditions or tests to be made will appear in this section. In limited-entry tables, all entries in this section will be in a simple question form that can be answered "yes" or "no."

**DETAB-X**   First decision table processor to be generally available. Results are COBOL.

**DETAB/65**   A decision table processor evolved from DETAB-X. It tests condition by condition; results are COBOL.

**ELSE rule**   Rule that acts as a catch-all for all rules not specifically covered in the table. Form varies according to the table processor used.

**Extended-entry table**   Table in which information normally expected in one quadrant may extend into another; that is, the stub area only names a condition or action; the entry portion gives it definition or value.

**FORTRAN**   Programming language; name derived from FORmula TRANslator.

**FORTAB**   A decision table processor developed by IBM, used with FORTRAN programs.

**Limited-entry table**   Table in which the quadrants are separate and distinct and information that normally appears in. one quadrant may not extend into another.

**Mixed-entry table**   Table that mixes the concepts of the limited entry and the extended entry. Although mixing may not occur on the same line, mixing of types of lines is permitted; one line in limited-entry format may be followed by a line in extended-entry format, and so on.

**Rule**   A single column of the decision table that shows the combination of responses to the conditions and the resulting or appropriate actions.

**Rule-by-rule testing**   A method of testing data against a decision logic table in order to ascertain which actions are appropriate. The data are put into the form of a rule column and then matched against the rule columns of the decision table until the matching rule is found. The appropriate actions can then be performed. The number of tests will range from one to the number of rules in the table.

**Rule header**    A series of numbers or alphabetic characters used to identify the individual rule columns of the table. The numbers are primarily for reference purposes.

**TAB40**    A decision table processor developed by Research Analysis Corporation. Tests are condition by condition; results are FORTRAN.

**TAB7C**    A decision table processor used at the U.S. Bureau of the Census. Tests are condition by condition; results are FORTRAN.

**Table header**    A means of identifying a table—a name or number. The header is placed above the condition-stub portion of the table.

**Table processor**    A software program that accepts decision logic tables as input and generates a compiler-language program as output. These outputs usually are FORTRAN or COBOL programs, which must be compiled in order to get a machine-language program.

**TABSOL**    A decision table processor developed by General Electric. Tests are condition by condition; results are COBOL.

# Appendix C

## Bibliography

Amerding, G. W., *FORTAB: A Decision Table Language for Scientific Computing Applications,* No. Rm-3306, RAND Corporation, September 1962.

Cantrell, H. N., King, J., and King, F. E. H., "Logic-Structure Tables," *Commun. ACM* (June 1961).

Dixon, P., "Decision Tables and Their Application," *Computers Automation* (April 1964).

Egler, J. F., "A Procedure for Converting Logic Table Conditions into an Efficient Sequence of Test Instructions," *Commun. ACM* (Sept. 1963).

Fife, R. C., "Decision Tables," *Proc. Univac Users Assoc.* (Spring 1966).

Fisher, D. L., "Data, Documentation and Decision Tables," *Commun. ACM* (Jan. 1966).

Grad, B., *Decision Tables in Systems Design,* ACM National Conference, September 1962.

Grad, B., "Tabular Form in Decision Logic," *Datamation* (July 1961).

Hawes, M. K., "The Use of Decision Tables for Problem Specifications," *Proc. Univac Users Assoc.* (Spring 1965).

Kavanagh, T. F., "TABSOL—The Language of Decision Making," *Computers Automation* (Sept. 1961).

Nickerson, R. C., "An Engineering Application of Logic-Structure Tables," *Commun. ACM* (Nov. 1961).

O'Brien, J. L., *Some Promising Approaches to Computerizing Administrative Operations,* U.S. Bureau of the Census (1964).

Pollack, S. L., "Analysis of the Decision Rules in Decision Tables," RAND Corporation, Memorandum RM-3660-PR, May 1963.

Pollack, S. L., *Detab-X: An Improved Business Oriented Computer Language,* RAND Corporation, 1962.

Schmidt, D. T., and Kavanagh, T. F., "Using Decision Structure Tables," *Datamation,* Pt. I (Feb. 1964); Pt. II (March 1964).

Vienott, C. G., "Programming Decision Tables in FORTRAN, COBOL or ALGOL," *Commun. ACM* (Jan. 1966).

———*Decision Logic Tables,* Bolling Air Force Base, Washington, D.C.

———*IBM 1401, Decision Logic Translator,* Form H20-0068, IBM Corp.

———*Decision Tables Education Guide,* Form R25-1684, IBM Corp. (1963).

———*Decision Tables—A Systems Analysis and Documentation Technique,* Form F20-8102, IBM Corp. (1962).

———*The Decision Language of the GE-225,* General Electric Computer Department, Phoenix, Ariz.

———*DETAB-X Preliminary Specifications for a Decision Table Structured Language,* Data Description and Transformation Logic Task Force of the CODASYL Systems Group, September 1962.

———*GE 225 TABSOL Manual,* No. CPB-147, General Electric Computer Department, Phoenix, Ariz., 1961.

———*TABSOL Application Manual—Introduction to TABSOL,* No. CPB-147A, General Electric Computer Department, Phoenix, Ariz. (1961).

———*DETAB/65 Preprocessor,* System Development Corp., SP-2534/000/00, July 7, 1966.

———*DETAB-X,* CODASYL Systems Group, 1962.

# Index